cupcakes
and
cashmere

at home

Editor: Rebecca Kaplan
Designer: Jenny Volvovski
Production Manager: Denise LaCongo

Library of Congress Control Number: 2014942738

ISBN: 978-1-4197-1583-9

Printed and bound in the United States
10 9 8 7 6 5 4 3 2 1

Abrams Image books are available at special discounts
when purchased in quantity for premiums and promotions
as well as fundraising or educational use. Special editions
can also be created to specification. For details, contact
specialsales@abramsbooks.com or the address below.

THE ART OF BOOKS SINCE 1949

115 West 18th Street
New York, NY 10011
www.abramsbooks.com

cupcakes
and
cashmere
at home

emily schuman

ABRAMS IMAGE, NEW YORK

THROUGHOUT MY LIFE, I've walked the fine line of being a homebody—not quite reclusive, but just happiest when I'm curled up on the sofa at home. This is no surprise, really, because I've always believed that your home is one of the clearest reflections of who you are. If I didn't find it to be far-and-away the most comfortable place to be, something must be wrong.

That feeling of home isn't about the big gestures either—the curtains, the rugs, the side chairs, and couches—it's about the well-loved books on the shelves, the tray for collecting keys on the table by the door, the smell of a familiar, much-loved dinner wafting out of the kitchen.

I'm an incredibly nostalgic person; and I have very fond memories of the house that I grew up in. I visit my parents all the time and am always secretly thrilled that nothing ever changes: There's no need to reset, or learn a new way. I still sit on the same stool at the kitchen counter while my dad cooks, marvel at the fog that rolls in each evening, and never tire of the James Taylor albums we've listened to countless times. It is wonderfully predictable, and it is home.

Growing up, my parents entertained all the time—as an only child, they'd let me pull a chair up to the table with their friends. Ultimately, I would fall asleep to the low hum of conversation. It wasn't just the music they played or the food they served, it was also about the people my parents invited in. It was a wonderfully complete world.

When my husband, Geoffrey, and I bought our first house late last year and set about assembling our first real home, the only thing we hoped to achieve was that same level of thoughtful and considered comfort. Sure, we hoped that our house would be beautiful, but more than that, we hoped that it would be our favorite place to be. This meant that while we could finally invest in a sofa that was the length and depth that we'd always wanted, we couldn't obsess when one of our three beloved cats decided to take her claws to it; we wouldn't ban red wine from our dinner parties; we wouldn't fixate over the imperfections of our flea market finds.

Our home is all about balance: No single aesthetic overrides the space (it's a mix of modern, vintage, and rustic), and no room skews too feminine or too masculine. We wanted a home that was serene and calm, but still playful—much like the outfits I wear, our home is classic with a bit of an edge . . . it's not precious and it's not too predictable. We're not trying to break new ground—instead we've focused solely on elevating the every day.

If you've spent time reading my blog, then you'll know that we love to have people over—for game nights, for themed parties, and for casual dinners. We tend to believe that an evening is successful when at least half of our guests have kicked off their shoes and are sitting around the coffee table on the floor (after all, that means that at least your rug is cozy). The success of our parties is the litmus test for us on whether we've created a home that's as warm and inviting as we intended.

When I sat down to figure out what this book about home should be, I knew I wanted to document the care and decision-making that went into every room. But I also knew that I couldn't do it without devoting at least half of the pages to entertaining—after all, what's the point in pouring your heart into your house if you don't get to share it with the people you love most.

Welcome to my happy place.

chapter

1

ENTRYWAY & LIVING ROOM

They say you can't make a first impression twice, right?

OUR HOUSE WAS BUILT IN 1916, and the original front door was still intact when we bought it, though it was painted an awkward color. Because we wanted to make a statement—and we wanted our home to feel unified and considered from the start—we painted the door a glossy black to tie in other elements of the house, including the fireplace, then we placed flanking kumquat trees on either side of the doormat in black, glossy planters. This makes up for the fact that our house does not have a proper entryway, per se—in fact, the front door opens onto a wide expanse that houses our living room on the right, our dining room on the left, and a view of the corner of our kitchen. Weirdly, even though L.A. is the land of perfect weather and the need for a coat closet and a place to stash wet shoes and umbrellas isn't exactly pressing, the lack of an entry hall or mudroom is actually kind of complicating. We really wanted to create a moment to mark the beginning of the house without blocking the flow of the space, either visually or physically. And, we wanted a place to stash the essentials.

Ultimately, when it came down to it, we had to reexamine what we considered to be essential and to counteract any tendencies to stash shoes and bags or procrastinate over opening our mail. Immediately to the left of the door, we placed a skinny little console table, a mirror (who wants to step out in the real world without checking their teeth for leftover lunch or stray lipstick?), and a ceramic dish that we got on our honeymoon in Italy. It's less than what we would have liked—and less than we thought we could live with—but it's actually been a helpful exercise in restraint.

We brought the same sense of utility and economy to our living areas: a more formal seating area and fireplace nook near the door and a TV room that's adjacent to the kitchen. The former is a little bit more done, while the TV room is marked by what is perhaps the world's most quicksand-like sofa (Geoffrey likes to joke that once I'm down, I'm out).

It took us a while to arrive at the right floor plans for both, since we wanted to turn both spaces into areas that we would actually use: Our house is not particularly large, and we don't have the luxury of only-for-special-occasions rooms, nor did we want those lifeless, dust-collecting zones in our home. We really wanted to maximize every square inch.

custom built-ins

gray malin artwork

leather sofa

brass sconces

otomi fabric

mid-century table

pillow combo

moroccan rug

the importance of

THE LAYOUT

////////////////////////////////

THERE ARE OH-SO-MANY WAYS to design and lay out a room—you can make it perfectly symmetrical, you can make it conversational, you can make it the antithesis of matchy-matchy. In determining the right mix, we settled on a combination of all three things, while taking into consideration those niggling little details, like what's the right distance between a couch and a coffee table (sixteen inches, for us) and whether every chair needs its own side table (we decided no). We also wanted to be sure that the lamps and side tables were at the right height, so that you can put your coffee cup down without either a precipitous drop or an awkward stretch, and so you don't find yourself so blinded by a lightbulb. Ultimately, it required some careful measuring, and we had to move past a few pieces that we loved, simply because they weren't the right dimensions. It was helpful to create a priority list (i.e., the couch was a must-have) and build from that.

From the start, we were very conscious of not overloading the rooms with furniture, particularly because we wanted pieces that were substantial and comfortable rather than airy and lightweight. The heavier the piece, the more it physically eats the space in all ways, and this is particularly true of items that cling to the floor. If you can't see the edges of the room, you tend to perceive it as smaller than it actually is. So, in lieu of buying all of the furniture against a floor plan, we went piece by piece, living with a new item for a few days before adding more. Ultimately, we ended up with less furniture than what was originally in the plan, which makes our rooms feel nice and airy rather than cramped.

FREE ONLINE LAYOUT RESOURCES

If you're not working with an interior designer and your space doesn't come with plans (although even those would be worth double-checking, just in case), there are some good resources for drawing your own. As you're measuring the space, be sure to take into account moldings along the floor, outlet placement, the width of doorways, which way the door opens, and where windows sit, as these factors can dramatically affect the workability of the space. (You also want to be sure that you'll be able to get your furniture pieces through your door!)

www.floorplanner.com
www.roomle.com

HOW TO CREATE AN ENTRYWAY
when you don't really have one

AS I'VE DISCUSSED, OUR ENTRYWAY—or lack thereof—presented its own unique challenges, namely, that if I had my druthers, I'd leave just about everything I need for a day by the door (and I like to kick off my shoes when I get home, too). Since there's no contained area, that simply isn't an option, and so I've had to retrain myself to carry the mail into the house and put my shoes away in the closet: Ultimately, it's a good thing, since if there were a closet available, I would quickly fill it. When we initially set about figuring out what we could do with the wall adjacent to the door, I had big plans: Maybe a pretty enameled hook or two for keys, the perfect lamp, a basket to catch umbrellas and shoes. But we ultimately resolved that less is more: Every lamp we tried couldn't breathe against the wall (the console we chose, which we found at HD Buttercup, is less than a foot wide; any wider would take up too much room), and every basket/catchall overwhelmed the space and created clutter. Ultimately, I'm thrilled that I've been retrained to actually put things away!

COFFEE TABLE
three ways

INVEST IN A GREAT COFFEE TABLE—and by invest, I don't necessarily mean that you have to spend a lot of money. Just be sure that you invest the time to find one that's the right size and the right height, since it's one of those pieces that is equal parts form and function: You want it to be pretty, but you want it to multitask as well. If you're not a coffee table person, then consider a collection of poufs and trays instead—this is a great solution if you're super short on space and need a scenario that can serve as extra seating, too.

I love a great coffee table vignette—I think it's the perfect place to create a little moment in a room that looks considered without being too precious.

polished feminine

1

california rustic

2

gilded floral

3

before

after

LITTLE MOMENTS *that go a* LONG WAY

You don't necessarily need to do a full-on remodel or furniture overhaul to make a room feel substantially different: Often, the smallest details can make a profound difference in how finished a space feels. Here are some quick fixes that deliver a lot of bang for the buck.

Paint the trim. I love a room whose trim is a slightly different shade than the wall; it gives the space extra dimension. Whether it's light gray against a slightly darker gray wall or a subtle white-on-white play, it adds texture. Also, baseboard (trim along the floor) tends to get scuffed, so a simple paint update can make a big difference.

Touch up scuffs with Fantastik. I learned this trick from a gallery owner and it totally works: A little bit of Fantastik on a paper towel removes dark marks, so you won't have to repaint.

Paint the ceiling a different color. This looks hands-down great—I like it when the shades are different enough for the shift to be noticed but still in the same family, i.e. pale gray paired with a gray that's 25 percent more saturated (in other words, you want to stay in the same paint card family).

Organize cords. This is a tedious task, but it's so worth it: A visible tangle of cords is just a bummer and can undo all of your work in making a room look pulled together.

Upgrade outlet covers. This is one of the cheapest fixes around: If your outlet covers are yellowing, cracked, or covered with old paint, bring in the new!

Swap lampshades. Just because a lamp comes with a predetermined shade doesn't mean that it has to stay that way! The photos on the opposite page show how we gave a standard lamp a makeover. Our lamp came with a dark brown shade that we swapped out for a white one.

Install dimmers. Good (i.e., flattering) lighting is everything, let's get real. We put dimmers everywhere.

Get curtains. I never thought I was one to fan out on curtains, but this experience has taught me that they should never be underestimated. They can completely soften a space, and if they're hung as close to the ceiling as possible, they can make the entire room feel bigger.

Rearrange the furniture. This doesn't need much of an explanation: A new layout can breathe entirely new air into a room and your stuff. You might come to fall in love with it all over again.

Reupholster a couch or chair. If that's not in the budget, consider getting an overly loved piece of upholstered furniture a good professional cleaning.

STREAMLINING THE CURTAIN DECISION-MAKING PROCESS

When I needed privacy in the past I always opted for more modern blinds. But working with Amber, our interior designer, opened my eyes to how transformational a vertical swathe of fabric can be. Curtains can be a big investment, though, particularly if you're having custom window treatments made. Unless large swatches are available, the best way to get a sense for the look and feel is to buy some yardage at a fabric store that's the color that you're thinking of. Then hold it up to the wall to get a sense of where you'd like them to hang (just above the window, really close to the ceiling, etc.) and how the color impacts the room. Once you've decided on a palette, then you can figure out how thick the fabric needs to be (if you're not interested in blocking out light, it doesn't really matter).

rug placement 101

WHO KNEW THAT THERE WAS A RULE to the placement of rugs? Well, it traditionally goes something like this: A properly spaced rug should end about 12 inches (30.5 cm) from the wall on every side. That lets your eye see where the wall and the floor connect, and it will allow your eye to see a rug as a rug, and not as a piece of carpet.

Rugs are expensive, though, which is why rug layering is so handy: If you have an area rug that's not nearly big enough to cover an expanse of floor, consider layering it over something utilitarian, like bound sisal carpet. Not only will it add a shot of texture, but it will give your budget a bit of room to stretch, too.

The biggest rule of rug buying, though, is to choose a textile that can withstand the amount of traffic you expect it to receive: If it's a runner in the entryway, it should be extra durable and very easy to clean. If it's a fragile dhurrie from an exotic vacation, maybe it deserves to be layered by the side of your bed, so it will only ever experience bare feet.

We made a conscientious effort—due to the facts that our house experiences a lot of foot traffic and we have three cats who like to pull at hooks in carpets—to spend wisely on rugs. As our family expands, I have no doubt there will be some baby food ground into the rugs at some point, too. We have three white, shaggy Moroccan-style rugs, none of which are priceless antiques: The nicest one is in our living room, the one in our bedroom was just over $100, and the family-room rug set us back about $600.

things to think about when rug shopping

Traffic. If you're shopping for a rug that's in one of the home's main thoroughfares, then go for something like sisal or a jute that can handle a lot of wear and tear. Also, pick something that you can easily replace without devastating your wallet. You don't want something that shows a clear pathway within the first year.

Likelihood of spills. Rugs in living rooms that are central to your cocktail party plans will likely get a dousing or two of red wine. Some patterns can easily camouflage little mishaps. Life is too short to obsess about keeping a silk champagne rug clean, so pick accordingly.

Budget. Rugs can get really expensive really fast. Consider layering a small (expensive) rug over a wool sisal or piece of bound carpet to help fill a room.

Pets and kids. If you have cats, and those cats have claws, beware of carpets with hooks that they'll invariably find totally tantalizing. Go for something that's cut up top or has a flat weave to dissuade them from pulling on it. If you have kids, or would like to have kids, don't pick something where food can be ground in (like a flokati)—easy to clean is key!

EMPTY WALLS
and what to do with them

AN EMPTY WALL can be pretty overwhelming, particularly if your art collection is small, but it's a great opportunity to not only showcase your sensibility but also make a major statement.

We've played with pretty much every approach, from a minimalist single picture to a gallery wall. Here are some tricks for each approach.

gallery wall

ASSEMBLING A VIGNETTE that actually hangs together (cliché intentional) is a little daunting—you don't want to put a bunch of holes in the wall only to realize that the entire thing is off-center.

I always start by coming up with a color palette and then stick to frames that are cohesive, for example, all white or all black. That way, you can make disparate elements—photos from childhood, framed quotes, collected objects, photographs—look like they belong together.

Before hanging anything, I arrange it on the floor first—it doesn't have to be perfect, but it gives me a good sense of where I should start and where the center should be. The trick is to start in the middle and then build out. You really need to get a good handle on the size of the space you're dealing with: Is it a cluster that will eventually expand, or are you looking to cover an entire wall in one fell swoop? If it's the latter, you'll need to measure it out carefully.

After arranging everything on the floor and measuring, I use tape to mark the proper placement of things on the wall, taking care to ensure that the larger pieces are scattered fairly evenly so that the wall doesn't quickly become lopsided.

why frames matter

WHILE I LIKE THE LOOK of cohesive frames, I shy away from framing everything in the same way—if it's too homogenous, it can cheapen the effect or make it look like you picked up every piece at the same store.

Some of the pieces on the wall have a mat, while others go right to the edge. It's the juxtaposition of some visually intense pieces with some that are softer and more subtle that makes the arrangement unique. While I tend to get things professionally framed with UV glass, this is something that can be done by hand. Ikea is a great resource for good, simple frames.

There are no hard and fast rules, so you should play around in the frame store and see what looks best—you might be surprised by how a simple frame can give something a totally new look.

And don't forget to consider the ultimate size you'd like the piece to be. A frame with a mat can make a tiny piece appear much more substantial.

UNEXPECTED THINGS TO PUT ON THE WALL

There's art, and then there are the simple things I've collected over the years that make our house feel more like a home. You can take anything and frame it really beautifully:

Drawings from childhood

Concert posters

Little mementos, like a cocktail napkin from your first date with your husband

Polaroids

Photo-booth strips

A favorite lyric typed up or painted (mine would be from Bob Dylan)

A framed speech, like the one from our wedding

Notes or cards that mean something to you

Something small made big, like a playing card or an envelope blown up into a huge print

A caricature from Times Square

AFFORDABLE ART RESOURCES

There are tons of amazing sites that specialize in afford-able art. These are some of my favorites:

20x200: They do editions of 200 for smaller prints, and they charge $20. As the edition numbers go down, the size and price go up. They have tons of great, modern photography, as well as wonderful illustrations.

Tappan Collective: The pieces here, which you can order in very large format, are a bit edgier, and they showcase artists from around the world.

Art Star: Airplanes shot from below, a woman crossing a plaza with a teetering pile of Hermès boxes, and beautiful shots of icebergs are just a handful of the offerings.

Society6: You can get the prints here pre-framed or get them emblazoned on iPhone cases.

Grey Area: Discover unique art objects like Chen & Kai's ham-hock coasters or Merijn Hos's wooden sculptures.

Mammoth & Co.: Here, you'll find Amber Ibarecche's prints of gems and Alexander Semenov's gorgeous pho-tos of jellyfish.

SINGLE PIECE *or* SYMMETRICAL HANG

THIS IS TRICKIER since winging it is usually a disaster—or, if not a disaster, then a big pain, since any visible holes must be spackled and repainted.

The trick is to measure from each side, from the ceiling, and from the floor—use a pen and use tape to ensure that it's perfect. Ultimately, artwork should be hung at eye level, though you might have to make adjustments to accommodate furniture (i.e., if a piece is going above a couch, it might look a bit strange if it's too elevated). Have a friend hold the piece in place so you can snap a picture and assess how it looks before you get the hammer out.

Perhaps most important: Hang your art last, after the room is completely arranged. If your curtains are bulky, you might want to center the piece using the edge of the curtain as the end of the wall. Again, have someone hold the piece in place so you can get a good sense of what feels right for the space.

all-time favorite book!

Scrabble letters spell out our last name

SURE, YOU CAN LINE UP all of your paperbacks arbitrarily—or you can geek out and order them according to the Dewey Decimal System (true story, I know someone who did this), but I've always done it by color. If you'll never be able to find your favorite novel unless you proceed alphabetically, this system is not for you, but I recognize books now by the design of their spine. It doesn't have to be a row-by-row rainbow, either; sometimes I mix it up by doing a vertical rainbow or color blocks throughout. The key is to mix in loved objects and treasures to add some extra texture and spots of interest.

BOOKSHELVES AREN'T JUST FOR BOOKS

I like to hang small pieces of art between stacks of books and then add in unexpected objects like a little dinosaur toy to make it more fun. We have a wooden wave that's actually a kid's toy in the blue section, along with various vacation memories, like a Día de los Muertos diorama from our anniversary trip to Mexico.

1 *mismatched patterns*

2 *eclectic brights*

3 *muted neutrals*

ONE COUCH
Three ways

A COUCH IS A BIG INVESTMENT: Not only are couches one of the more expensive pieces of furniture, but they're also among the largest. The most important thing is the obvious thing: Make sure you spend a lot of time sitting on the couch of your choice, to ensure that it's comfortable, that it's the appropriate depth, that you can fit as many people on it as you would want. Not only is it wasteful to chuck a couch into a landfill, but they're so hard to move in and out that once it's home, you want it to stay home.

I always go for a solid-colored couch, even if it's in an unexpected color—you can add color and texture through pillows and blankets and give it a totally different look. I like to mix up the supporting textiles every six months to a year—it can make a room feel completely new again.

If you don't have the budget for the couch of your dreams, consider reupholstering something you already own (or a hand-me-down). Reupholstering isn't cheap, but it's a great way to give an item a new lease on life. If Ikea is the only budget-friendly contender, consider customizing it ever so slightly with PrettyPegs, an ingenious company that creates colorful feet for Ikea furniture.

DESIGNING WITH PETS IN MIND

Readers often ask me if I keep the cats in mind when I make decorating decisions. Quite frankly, the cats are always on my mind—I'm obsessed with them! But that said, I don't let them dictate too much when it comes to interior decor. I know that they're going to go at our upholstery every once in a while, and that's something I've come to live with.

The biggest deterrent has been to give them their own cat tower, since they love to get up high. Granted, ours is not the *Downton Abbey* of cat towers—it's huge and it's ugly. I have fantasies about getting some Persian rugs from Pier 1 and reupholstering the entire thing.

RENTING

1

Don't spend too much on site-specific furniture. In our last apartment, we bought a console that was perfect—to the quarter inch—for the space. And quite frankly, we probably should have left it there because it isn't the right dimensions for our house. If you're going to acquire nice things, invest in chairs, lamps, and side tables, which are more easily integrated into any space.

2

Don't invest in permanent storage: Maybe install one single shelf at the entryway, but otherwise get creative with something like a vintage crate or a wire basket to catch kicked-off shoes and umbrellas. Look for pretty and portable accessories for storage, like enamel hooks for bags and scarves and a nice tray for keys. You can always use those elsewhere. In the living room, this is a good time to use a bookshelf, as built-ins are not a reality for a rental (unless you can get your landlord to fund them).

3

Invest in a nice mirror for the entryway: It can always go from your apartment to your first home, and seeing as it's the first thing people see when they enter, and the last thing people look at when they leave, it's worthy of some budget.

4

If you're nervous about investing in an expensive coffee table, consider a group of poufs with trays on top or layering smaller coffee tables together. You can then break them apart and use them throughout your new space.

5

Great art is everything, so start your collection now. You don't have to spend a fortune by any means, but pieces found over the years generally tell a better story than one long session on the computer sourcing art to fill a new home.

6

Spackling and repainting is really easy and can be done in an afternoon; you can totally do it yourself. I've never been in an apartment that didn't have a shoddy paint job—it's just par for the course (you can also replace the switch plates, etc., which takes two seconds and makes a big difference).

7

Focus on accessories like throw pillows, dishes, and trays. You can buy a really crappy coffee table and put a gorgeous tray on it, and nobody will know what's underneath.

OWNING

1

Consider building in storage, particularly if your home lacks a coat closet. Since we live in Los Angeles, this isn't a priority, but in any city where there's inclement weather, the overwhelm of coats, boots, and umbrellas can quickly swamp your entryway.

2

Invest in pieces that fit perfectly, whether it's a standing lamp, a console table, or a chair in the corner. These are functional pieces that will be there forever (or at least as long as you own the house!).

3

Wallpaper your entry—or paint it a separate color. Spend the money and time to make this space feel really special so that entering and exiting your home is an event.

4

This is a good time to invest in shelving, particularly as a way to eliminate clutter or any extra furniture on the floor, as it can look kind of junky to have too many bookcases.

5

Invest in a high-quality couch that fits perfectly—you don't have to spend a fortune, but make sure that it's really comfortable and sound enough that you can reupholster it as your taste changes without having to start over.

6

Hire professional painters, even if you think your paint job is simple. It should be perfect. And while they're at it, consider contrasting the ceiling or the molding or the trim—even if it's in a subtle way. Paint your entryway door and make a statement.

chapter

//////////////////////// 2 ////////////////////////

DINING ROOM

//

farrow & ball
hague blue
wall color

layered kilim &
jute rugs

sputnik
chandelier

glass bar cart

white painted
Table

pink velvet
chairs

the importance of
ENTERTAINING

////////////////////////////////

HAVING A PROPER DINING ROOM to entertain in is kind of a dream come true, if only because entertaining is one of my very favorite things to do. Having a dedicated zone isn't a requirement, though, as I first started having friends over when I lived in a tiny apartment—we would huddle around the coffee table for meals. But it's so nice to be able to set a real table, with flowers and china and maybe a candle or two thrown in for good measure.

While G and I do love to put on a dinner party, we also like to have more than our fair share of low-key meals at home. We often gravitate to the stools around our kitchen counter, but we've set a household rule that we're not allowed to eat in front of the TV . . . unless it's awards season, the Olympics, or World Cup time. If we put more than ten minutes of effort into making a meal, then we take the extra thirty seconds to set the dining room table and really have dinner—this was a tradition when I was growing up, and those times spent catching up with my parents after busy days are some of my fondest memories. I'm so glad they made the time for me, and so, in turn, G and I try to make that time for each other. We think of it as the beginning

of what will hopefully be many family traditions—once a high chair is involved, some might be messier than others.

Dining rooms are tricky spaces because they can easily veer into the world of formality, where you feel silly eating eggs at the table in your pajamas. Finding that line between *eat-in* and *nice-enough-to-host-your-boss-to-dinner* is really difficult. We think we have solved it, adding some fancy-seeming flourishes while focusing on comfort as the unifying theme that holds the room together: Comfortable layered rugs underneath, and comfortable chairs that encourage hours of lounging.

We also took durability into consideration, since there's no fun in hosting a dinner party when you're concerned that your guests are going to tip their red wine onto the floor and cause hundreds of dollars worth of destruction.

While we did choose to have a couple of rugs underfoot—the vintage one I fell in love with was smaller than we needed, so we layered it on top of a sisal rug. All in all, I think we found the perfect balance between cozy and formal, everyday-appropriate and overly rarified.

LIGHTING FIXTURES

ONE OF THE FIRST THINGS we did when we moved into our house was swap out a majority of the lighting fixtures. I love a great pendant lamp—it's really the first opportunity you have to make a major statement in a new home. And you don't have to spend a lot of money to do it: Retailers like West Elm, Ikea, and CB2 have so many great ones, plus there's always the option of picking up a vintage or antique chandelier (and having it rewired, if necessary). While most pendants have to live relatively close to the ceiling to stay well out of the way (and disperse light correctly), the dining room is one place where a lighting fixture can hang lower and make a bit more of a statement, as the table blocks the path anyway.

To that end, you can hang a light really low, particularly if it's somewhat transparent and the light is diffuse—a single pendant shining directly down won't light the room properly if it's too close to the surface of the table. A good rule of thumb is to create at least a few feet of clearance and then pick a lamp that isn't a spotlight, unless you're placing a series of pendant lamps that will spread the light around—a grouping, maybe three, equally spaced across the length of your table. To figure out what looks best, put the table in place and then have someone hold the light at various heights.

three ways

TO SET

a pretty table

I LIKE TO PUT A LOT OF THOUGHT into both the table settings and the tablescape when we entertain. You don't want the design to compete with your food; rather, it should be the perfect complement. Putting together little moments like this is one of my main outlets for creative expression (I'm not a painter, after all), so I always use it as an opportunity to have fun and try new things. Whether it's creating mini arrangements for every place setting or scattering flowers down the center of the table, you can play it pretty much any way you want. I just try to match the degree of formality to the setting (e.g., a stemless wine glass for more casual dinners, pretty china for girly brunches).

1 girls' brunch

- Floral/vintage china
- Cake stands/bowls for serving treats
- Champagne in ice bucket + coffee in a French press
- Ceramic baskets of berries for shots of color
- Bud vases for roses to scatter around the table

2 Takeout

- Remove all food from boxes and put on trays/bowls
- Use silverware instead of plastic utensils
- Keep it casual with bottles of beer
- Small, unscented candles
- Tight floral arrangements in mason jars

3 formal dinner

- Use a runner or tablecloth with matching napkins
- Have place cards at each seat
- Keep the table sparse with the food as the centerpiece
- Place wine in a decanter and water in a pitcher
- Light tall, unscented candles to scatter around the table

BAR CART

OUR BAR CART IS A BIG FOCAL POINT in our dining room: Not only is it physically significant (it's not a particularly large room), but it's also usually packed to the rafters with alcohol (what can we say . . . we like to drink!). I usually restyle it to fit the affair when I have company over, particularly if we're doing a signature cocktail. This can make things easier to plan for, too, as it's always disappointing to guests when they spy a bottle of Vodka only to be told that you forgot to get tonic! If you don't have a bar cart, poke around at flea markets and local yard sales. eBay usually has a great selection, too, as does Society Social, an adorable website dedicated to the art of entertaining. I bought our first bar cart at the Melrose Trading Post and it was originally intended for science labs. It had such a cool industrial feel, though, that it transitioned nicely as a bar cart. Since it was a bit too rustic for our new space, it now lives outside and holds a collection of succulents. But the main point is not to think too literally here. There are a lot of unique pieces that will look great when dressed up with pretty bottles of alcohol.

THE PERFECT BAR CART

Plymouth Gin
Rittenhouse Rye
Stolichnaya Vodka
El Charro Tequilla Silver
Carpano Antica Vermouth
Angostura bitters
Club Soda
Tonic
Ginger Ale
Luxardo Cherries
Fresh Lemons and Limes

AFFORDABLE WINES TO BUY BY THE CASE

Ronco Blanchis Pinot Grigio
Domaine Les Pins Bourgueil Rosé
Ancient Peaks Winery Margarita Vineyard
Renegade (red blend)

bar cart essentials

champagne flute

martini glass

wine glass

collins glass

high ball

*bar cart
every day*

bar cart
entertaining

RENTING

1

Get cheap chairs: They don't even have to be the same. You can throw pillows on them, or paint them the same color to make them look more cohesive and fancier than they actually are.

2

Consider investing in a bench for one side instead of a ton of chairs you might not need. In our last apartment, we had a bench on one side and chairs on the other—it allowed us to squeeze more people in at dinner parties. And then when we moved, we were able to use the bench at the foot of our bed (though they're often great in an entryway, or even outside).

3

Start collecting china and serving pieces—if you have a specific aesthetic in mind that's signature to your personality, they'll always work, even as your homes evolve.

4

We never spent a lot on our dining room table (our old table is now our outdoor table). You can always dress a table up with a tablecloth when guests come over, or give it a nice paintjob.

5

If you'd like to make an investment, consider a table with leaves—if it's not the right scale in your new place, it might work as a breakfast table.

6

Get a bar cart! They're so festive and can fit in with any home. They occupy a small footprint and are a good way to conceal an unsightly corner. We spent $50 on our first bar cart (it was originally a science cart). It's too industrial for our space now, so it lives outside and holds plants, though it would have worked well as a storage unit in a bathroom.

OWNING

1

This is the time to invest in a really gorgeous table, particularly if you have a busy aesthetic and all the other surfaces in your home or covered. It can be nice to have a beautiful, clear, open table.

2

Think about adding a credenza to your dining room, particularly if you have the space. It makes it so much easier to entertain, and it's always nice to have extra storage, particularly if it means that you can free up some of your kitchen cabinets.

3

Invest in chairs that are really, really comfortable so when you entertain, guests are inclined to linger—people will want to stay around the table and drink wine and play board games. (If there's upholstery involved, Spray Guard it.)

4

Get one set of really nice linens—a table runner, place mats, napkins—along with stemware and silver for special occasions. It's nice to mark holidays and other occasions as special and bust out the good stuff!

chapter

//////////////// 3 ////////////////

KITCHEN

//

brass
fixtures

brass
hardware

white
subway
tile

colorful
kilim
rug

dolomite
slab

organic
modernism
walnut
barstools

the importance of
OPEN SPACE

///////////////////////////////

LIKE EVERYONE ELSE in the Los Angeles metropolitan area, we put a beautiful, open kitchen at the very top of our wish list when were house hunting. The lack of one (or of the option to install one) was a deal breaker. And they can be elusive.

Outside of the word *open*, though, the essential qualities of a kitchen you want to cook in are kind of nebulous. Clean, bright, nice appliances, ample counter space, sure. But it's about so much more than that. In my mind, the perfect kitchen is a room that feels welcoming and cozy.

When we first visited what is now our home, the kitchen was my first stop—and I didn't want to leave, which I took to be a great sign. While we've given it a pretty minor face-lift (more below), its vaulted ceiling and dimensions felt pretty perfect.

As you might imagine, Geoffrey and I cook a lot—for each other, for the blog, and for friends. And we often like to cook simultaneously (G does most of the cooking, while I handle the baking), which means that we needed a kitchen spacious enough to accommodate both of us without us crashing into each other with hot pans and messy dishes. The space is big, but perhaps even more important is the fact that every inch of the kitchen is well used, which is integral to the flow of the space and its organization.

What's more, the island easily allows for four stools (they're from Organic Modernism and are substantial yet sleek), so it's easy to keep each other company if only one pair of hands is needed to prep dinner. And, as we all know, when you entertain, everyone likes to hang out in the kitchen while you finish up the meal, so it's nice that people can sit and hang out rather than hover.

There are a few other moments that make the layout of our kitchen work really well, and I'd highly recommend taking these into consideration if you're house hunting or thinking about a renovation. Our fridge is well positioned near the center island, which allows us to unload things quickly and easily. The kitchen has two sinks—a big one for washing dishes, etc. in front of the window and a smaller one in the middle of the island, directly across from the stove.

Fortunately, the island was already plumbed and the major appliances were well-placed, which saved us money and time. Except for the slab of dolomite on the island, most of our upgrades cost us very little, whether it was swapping in new drawer pulls, opting not to have a hanging pendant (the track lighting was more than sufficient), or changing the window treatments. Those small tweaks left us with the kitchen of our dreams—one that we'll be happily cooking in for years to come.

DISPLAYING SPOONS

////////////////////////////////

THE RULE IN THE KITCHEN is that if something is going to be out permanently, it has to be pretty. To that end, I searched high and low for marble canisters to hold a handful of spatulas and mixing spoons by the stove. We found these at Crate and Barrel and bought an extra, just in case one should crack or break—it's so perfect, I'd be heartbroken if something happened to it and I didn't have a replacement!

DIY WOODEN UTENSILS

We've never spent a lot of money on kitchen tools (you really just don't have to)—generally, the more basic they are the better they function. I stock up on simple wooden mixing spoons (you can buy a bunch of them for a few dollars) since they look great when grouped together in a canister and you can never have too many lying around. They're also the ideal blank canvas for adding a touch of color. I gave mine a little makeover by dipping the ends in different shades of pink paint for a sort of ombré-inspired nod to the kitchen. I simply added some painter's tape, painted the ends and set them out to dry. The set in my kitchen turned out so well that I made several extras and gave them as gifts. Wrap a grosgrain ribbon around a grouping (I think five is the perfect amount), package them up in a cellophane bag with a matching hand towel, and you have a beautiful little present!

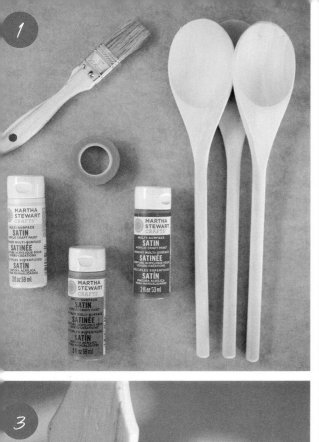

elevating the everyday
IN THE KITCHEN

////////////////////////////

WHILE ONE CAN INARGUABLY NEVER have too many kitchen towels, I became pretty obsessive about finding the right details for the kitchen. As Geoffrey will tell you, I fixated on everything from the hand soaps at the kitchen sink (I believe in finding a signature scent, after all!) to the rug in front of the sink. Because the room is so simple, every little thing makes a pretty big statement.

In the kitchens of my past, which were far from photogenic, the small things made a huge difference, too. Just having a pretty hand soap on the kitchen sink (with the dish soap and sponges stored away beneath) can give even a cruddy sink a makeover. And a bright little rug can cheer up a chipped tile floor. A friend even wallpapered her old fridge to give it a face-lift (it was a beater)—genius!

DIY
SPICE JAR
organization

WHEN THE POWERS THAT BE went about packaging spices, they didn't do a great job of thinking through all the ways those spices might be stored and used (not to mention that I always seem to have approximately nine different brands of spices in all different shapes and sizes). I was never too picky about it in the past, but when we moved, I took the opportunity to finally consolidate spices and get them in order. I found a homogenous type of bottle to house them in and labeled them consistently. If you're even a tiny bit compulsive, this is the sort of project that brings an insane amount of satisfaction! Plus, it's been infinitely easier to find what I've needed since they're now also all organized alphabetically (this is clutch when you're in the middle of baking a cake and have flour on your hands and don't want to dig).

before

pumpkin pie
spice

cream of
tartar

juniper
berries

cinnamon
sticks

ground
allspice

ground
nutmeg

vie
c

thyme

new mexico
chili powder

celery
salt

co

chili
powder

bay

labeling

basil leaves

bay
leaf

ground
cardamom

ground
cloves

coriander
seeds

creole
seasoning

ground
ginger

herbes de
provence

juniper
berries

black
peppercorn

white
pepper

poppy
seed

after

PANTRY

organization

////////////////////////////

I'VE ORGANIZED MY PANTRY in pretty much the opposite way to what you'll find at the typical grocery store. The junk food (i.e., Thin Mints . . . I think I keep the Girl Scouts in business) is out of reach on the bottom shelf, while the things I need most frequently are readily accessible.

I should have a rewards card at the Container Store because I spent one-hundred-plus hours (and many more dollars) there during the move, figuring out ways to maximize our space without adding unnecessary clutter (if organizational systems aren't suited to how you actually use a space, they sometimes just get in the way). I added some extra shelves here and there and a couple of lazy Susans for cabinets that I can't see into (it's nice to give them a twirl for vinegars and whatnot that you might use only rarely).

In our pantry, I've grouped everything by theme. Baking soda, baking powder, chocolate chips, and other baking supplies are located near each other; meal essentials like Arborio rice, tomato sauce, and dried pasta are in another area; while more obscure ingredients, like pine nuts and dried apricots, are a little more out of the way.

fridge organization

IT USED TO FEEL LIKE I spent the better part of an hour looking for things in the fridge (it's that experience where you can't see the things that are right in front of you). And so I made the decision to create some pretty basic organization systems in the fridge, to maximize both space and time, and it's made a huge difference.

LaCroix sparkling water just might be my favorite thing in the world, and it takes up a ton of space. Instead of plopping a carton in there and giving it half a shelf, we now put the cans in an actual soda holder. I also bought a pretty egg crate at Anthropologie that accomplishes two things: One, it pretties it up in there, and two, I can see with a quick glance whether we're getting low on eggs, which is key if you're a big baker. I'm also far less likely to fumble it than I would a carton.

We've established the very simple rule of putting the things that are going to expire first near the front, which is key, thanks to my extreme cottage cheese addiction. Then, there's an overall hierarchy that makes it easier to find things. Beverages go on the bottom shelf; quick meals, leftovers, and snacks like hummus go at eye level, so they're available for grab and go; and things that should be properly stored (like cheese and vegetables) get tucked away in their respective drawers.

Every Sunday night, I quickly go through it all and toss anything that might be bad, freshening it up and taking stock in the same five minutes.

before   *after*

RENTING

1

Cover up crappy looking appliances: You can even wallpaper your fridge (just use rubber cement, as it's easy to remove).

2

Swap out knobs with prettier enamel options (Anthropologie does really nice ones)—just remember to save the originals so you can replace them when you move out!

3

Invest in nice canisters, which you can use as display on your countertops—this is key for concealing unsightly corners (or, if they're really ugly, your countertops)!

4

If storage is tight, get a metal rack for the wall to hold knives—they look nice and streamlined, and you can always use it in your next house.

5

Expand storage space in your cabinets with lazy Susans and in-cabinet shelves: The Container Store has this stuff in spades, and it can really make a huge difference if space is tight.

6

If space is really tight, get a metal shelving unit from Uline. They look industrial, which means weirdly that they go with almost any aesthetic, and they're sturdy enough to hold heavy pots and pans.

7

Get floor pads by the sink, particularly if you don't have a dishwasher and will be standing there for hours doing dishes after a dinner party.

8

Dress up your sink with pretty hand soaps and lotion (make sure to choose products that are not too scented, as you don't want them to impact the taste of your food!).

9

Drawer liners are essential if you're living in a rental, particularly because they're easy to install and don't cost a lot of money!

10

Get an oven thermometer and check your oven before you start baking—350 degrees in the oven in our rental was actually 425. I burned a lot of cakes before I figured it out!

OWNING

1

Figure out which appliance matters to you the most. We inherited an amazing (and unused!) range with our home, otherwise that would have been top priority. If you never cook, invest in a fridge that has tons of storage space for takeout and prepared meals, and get a dishwasher that's top of the line.

2

We replaced the sinks in our kitchen, so we bought very basic and classic designs in chrome and then had them plated. Gold and brass sinks are really, really expensive, and the color is rarely right (it can go orange or rose gold), and so we plated them to save a huge amount of money (and to get the shade we wanted).

3

We kept some of our countertops and swapped others (it would have been way too expensive to do them all). We kept the black countertops around the perimeter of the kitchen, but then did a custom island. We chose dolomite, because it looks like marble, but it's more durable: It has the same light, clean look but it doesn't etch or show stains.

4

Invest in really good lighting. Our kitchen had such good lighting that we took out the original light fixture in the middle and didn't replace it. If you aren't so lucky, consider putting good track lighting in so that you can really see what you're doing in the kitchen!

5

Sometimes things that seem convenient are actually not useful. Our original kitchen had a desk, which I thought was an amazing get, but then, when I thought about it, I realized I wouldn't actually be sitting there reading cookbooks, as we have a million other places in the house for sitting and working. Instead, we raised the desk a bit higher and created enough room below for a wine fridge.

6

Build out more storage so that you can get as much off your counters as possible—and within your cabinets, consider customizing them: We have a built-in section for knives that's amazing, as well as vertical slates for cutting boards and baking sheets.

chapter

////////////////////// 4 //////////////////////

BEDROOM

//

grey otomi
print
shades

white canopy
bed

colorful
pillows

mid-century
side Tables

moroccan
wedding
blanket

star
pendant

beni ourain rug

wood bench

the importance of
COMFORT

////////////////////////////

WHILE IT'S EASY to make a bedroom an afterthought—it's hidden from public view, it's dominated by a gigantic piece of furniture, you only sleep in it—it's essentially at the center of self-care and a good reflection of how well you tend to yourself. It's so, so easy to let it go: Often, we'll forget to make the bed, or our bedside tables will be subsumed by Kleenex boxes and books, because nobody else is really going in there. But paying attention to the little things and taking the time to put stuff away really, really matters. There's nothing worse than to be tired after the end of a long day and walk into a world of chaos. Having a beautiful, peaceful bedroom is a giant step toward ensuring that you can start your days on the right foot.

In the process of putting together any home, one of the more instructive things to do is to spend several weeks collecting images of rooms that you respond to or find calming. Without thinking about it at all, start tearing out and compiling anything that catches your attention, and when you have a good mass of interiors, start to identify what they have in common. For me and G, it was pale shades of color and huge swathes of white—with a few colorful splashes of color thrown in for good mea-

sure—that repeatedly caught our eye. Clearly, we were drawn to clean and calm spaces, and we used that as a map for our dream bedroom.

The comfort of a bedroom is directly related to the comfort of your bed, and so we spent a long time wandering the floors of department stores trying out beds (won't bore you with the details). My first instinct was to just guess and order one online during mattress sale time (almost every holiday weekend), but G insisted that we put in the time to see them in person and I'm so glad we did.

Once we'd taken care of some of the more tactical (read: boring) decisions, I switched my focus to the important stuff, that is, finding the perfect white bedding and accent moments. Amber, our interior decorator, had the brilliant idea of using Otomi fabric to reupholster our bedside lamps (genius), and we found a Moroccan wedding blanket to accent the foot of the bed. We also made the (at the time) brave decision to use the windows in our bedroom as the headboard. For whatever reason, I'd always been schooled in the idea that a bed must be against a solid wall, but to do that in our space would have ensured a really awkward use of the room. And I've come to love having the morning light streaming in when we wake up.

making a
PEACEFUL
BEDROOM

FOR A HOME THAT'S RENDERED in a very neutral palette of grays and whites, we spent an inordinate amount of time figuring out the perfect colors. Paint color is kind of everything: Not only does it set the tone for every room, and by extension, the entire house, but it can turn a space warm or cold and the light flattering or harrowing.

While we didn't want every room to feel like it had stepped out of a single catalog—and we mixed periods and styles throughout the house as an antidote to sameness and things being too matchy-matchy—we did want it to feel cohesive. The best way to ensure that it felt like it all belonged to the same home was to restrain the palette to a handful of shades. Besides the palette, a few other moments—bright accent colors and some lighting fixtures that are repeated throughout the home—tie the house together. But it really comes down to selecting the right paint.

We tested a lot of whites and grays—in all, we probably sampled at least twenty, if not thirty. It's so important to paint an adequate swatch and then see how the color changes and morphs as the natural light works its way throughout your house over the course of a day (not to mention one color in a certain room can look entirely different in another part of the house).

Some grays looked too purple or brown and some were too pale; ultimately, we settled on colors that all work really well together, even though some are relegated to the front of the house while others are in the bedrooms and offices.

RULES OF THUMB FOR COLOR PALETTES

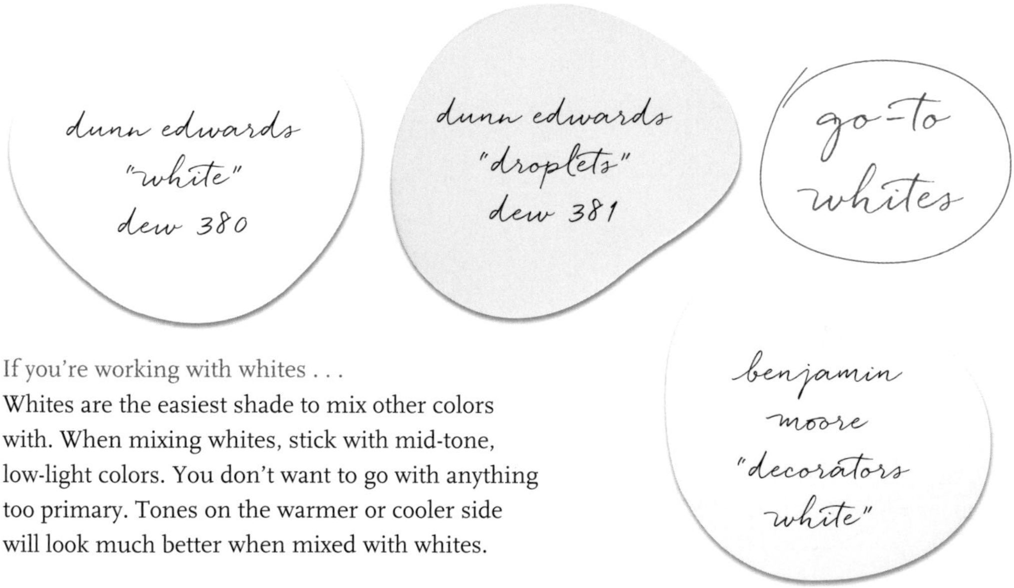

dunn edwards
"white"
dew 380

dunn edwards
"droplets"
dew 381

go-to
whites

benjamin
moore
"decorators
white"

If you're working with whites . . .
Whites are the easiest shade to mix other colors
with. When mixing whites, stick with mid-tone,
low-light colors. You don't want to go with anything
too primary. Tones on the warmer or cooler side
will look much better when mixed with whites.

perfect palette grays

benjamin moore "classic gray"

dunn edwards "charcoal smudge" dew 6370

dunn edwards "faded gray" dew 382

If you're working with grays and taupes (our palette) . . .
Grays and taupes look best with cool and earthy tones mixed in. You don't want to go with anything too jarring. Stick with complementary accents.

farrow & ball "hague blue"

benjamin moore "reflection"

love color? try these

dunn edwards "vanilla blush" dew

If you're working with brights . . .
Keep everything else neutral and light. Whites and tans vibe well with bold and bright colors.

the appeal of symmetry

BECAUSE WE WANTED OUR bedroom to be as calm and relaxing as possible, we minimized the distractions—and with this came the search for symmetry. We chose matching bedside tables and matching bedside lamps. There are a million other ways to play this, though. In lieu of a bedside table, you can use a Moroccan pouf (if you want it to serve as a table, you can top it with a sturdy tray), a vintage chair, mismatched tables, or even a big stack of coffee table books. Ultimately, you just want to make sure that you have enough square footage to store your essentials, including a reading lamp (unless you opt for a swing arm from the wall, or a floor lamp).

The main thing to keep in mind is that you want to be able to reach everything easily (alarm clock, water, book) and you want to create a bedside table that won't topple when hit with a pillow or, in my case, when prodded by a curious cat, so make sure it's sturdy!

maximizing the walls

AS MENTIONED, I've historically only ever put the head of my bed against a solid wall—but due to the room's layout, the bed really only worked centered underneath a wall of windows, which we ultimately came to embrace. Amber installed a soft white curtain, which in some ways creates the illusion of a solid wall while also adding a really nice shot of texture. Honestly, I can't imagine having the room any other way—it still feels cozy and protected, but the natural light is incredible, too.

using texture for comfort

QUITE FRANKLY, nothing is better—or in my mind, more mood-establishing—than swinging your legs out of bed and finding something soft and warm underfoot. I prioritized finding the right bedside rug above almost everything else in the room, if only because I wanted it to feel perfect—cozy and welcoming, and wonderfully plush. We chose a sort of subdued shag rug, though a great flokati or sheepskin (Ikea has great faux ones) works really well, too.

things that guarantee
GOOD SLEEP

1   Move the TV out of the bedroom. While this necessitates relocating to the couch when one of us has the flu and needs a day napping in front of the TV, we find that we get way more sleep when we can't switch on *The Tonight Show* or *Colbert*. I could probably watch TV all night long if given the option.

2   Install blackout shades. Sometimes you need to sleep in beyond sunrise, and the way to achieve this (outside of checking in to a hotel) is through blackout shades. They're worth the investment.

3   Use dimmers at every light switch. It's much more low-key to get prepped for bedtime in low light than to go from full-on to lights out.

4   Invest in a quality mattress that will last you a good decade.

5   Wear an eye mask. Dorky, sure, but these are a total necessity, particularly if your significant other tends to stay up reading.

6   Maintain a low-key color palette. As discussed, keeping the shades limited to soft taupes, grays, and whites is calming and relaxing.

7   Keep a stash of great novels (or an iPad) nearby. I love to fall asleep while reading. If my brain is racing or I'm feeling anxious about work, reading is the fastest way to calm my mind and knock myself out.

8   Set the right temperature. They say that people sleep best when it's slightly cool. That's definitely my preference. I like to actually need the weight of the blankets, and there's nothing worse than a sweaty sleep!

WHEN I WAS YOUNG, my mom had to practically force me to make my bed each morning. It seemed like such an enormous task that early in the day, but now that I'm an adult, I have a new appreciation for the chore. It's the easiest way to do something productive minutes after waking up, not to mention that slipping into a well-made bed at night is one of life's little luxuries.

Beyond making the bed each morning, I'm pretty specific about how I like it to look. Instead of just having a fitted sheet with a duvet on top (how I did things all through college and for the majority of my twenties), our setup's now a bit more involved. On top of the fitted sheet, I now use a flat sheet, something I used to find intrusive since it would

inevitably end up tangled at the bottom of the bed by midnight. I'm still what Geoffrey calls an *active sleeper*, so I have the tendency to thrash around, but when the flat sheet is properly tucked into the bottom of the bed, I can't dislodge it in the same way. On top of the flat sheet, we have a light coverlet, which not only looks nice when the bed is made but also provides the perfect amount of weight during the night. We keep a heavier blanket in a duvet folded neatly at the bottom of the bed, so should it get cold, it's easy to pull up even when we're half asleep. We each have two sleeping pillows (I love a half-down, half-feather mix), and when the bed is made, we finish it with three throw pillows to complete the look.

diy lighting

THERE ARE MANY wonderfully affordable lamps out there (plus a host of great vintage options on sites like eBay, 1stdibs, and Etsy), but as is often the case, we fell in love with a pair that needed a little bit of work. So Amber had the brilliant idea of upgrading the lampshade to make them perfect. Using embroidered Otomi fabric purchased on our anniversary trip to Mexico, we reupholstered the shades, which, while not super cheap, turned them into something pretty unique and special. We also considered lining the inside of the lamp with a colored or metallic paper, and I've had success in the past with changing the base, either by painting it (or spray painting it, actually, which is a common prop stylist's trick) or wrapping it in something like sisal or rope (glue gunning it together along the way). If you want a super-simple update, trim a very basic lampshade with grosgrain ribbon. Small touches can make a huge difference.

decoding bulb brightness

AS YOU'RE PROBABLY WELL AWARE, the light-bulbs that we all grew up with are being phased out of the market, and while I'm all about earth-friendly options, it can be hard to find bulbs that satisfy environmental standards while still emitting a warm light. Fortunately, the options are improving every year. As discussed throughout the book, you won't find many light switches in our house that aren't actually dimmers—it's so nice to be able to dial down the light as needed.

Pendant Lights: We use chrome-dipped bulbs, since these reflect light back into the fixture and allow it to disperse throughout the room. Chrome-dipped bulbs are generally low wattage (40W), so we use floor lamps to fully light the room.

Bedside Tables: We use 38W bulbs: enough to light our respective sides of the bed without turning bedtime into a less-than-relaxing situation. These are also on dimmers.

Living Room Lamps: Here, we amp it up a bit with 60W bulbs, which give a lot of light—if we need more, I'd rather turn on more floor lamps than invest in brighter bulbs.

CLOSET
organization

//

THERE'S NOT MUCH of a point to investing in a wardrobe if you can't see your clothing well enough to actually wear it. While I have a pretty expansive closet (in terms of quantity, not rack space), I still try to go through my clothing seasonally and move out anything that I haven't worn at least once.

If something is special or has sentimental value, it might go into storage, but if I think I can live without it, or it's starting to fade or show signs of age (or stains), then it goes to Goodwill.

To make the separation easier, I'll usually pack clothing that I'm on the fence about in a suitcase or duffel, and then store it in the back of my closet. Three to six months later, I'll open it back up to see if I've actively missed anything. More often than not, I can't believe I was ever attached and am ready to move it out of the house.

Which leaves us with the pieces that are staying. Call me compulsive, but I find that if I invest the time in organizing my closet fastidiously at the outset, it's much easier to maintain. You'll easily be able to see the empty hanger and put the item back where you found it. When I don't start with a system, it becomes unmitigated chaos very quickly. So here are my basic closet organization rules.

1   Take everything out of the closet. Rent some rolling racks if necessary (particularly for valuable dresses, or anything that might wrinkle).

2   Invest in uniform hangers—I like any that are velour (like Huggable Hangers), since they are compact and clothing stays put.

3   Try everything on, checking in the mirror for anything that might need to be cleaned or repaired before putting it in your closet. Invite a (stylish and forthright) friend over to help—sometimes it's useful to have an honest second opinion about whether something is flattering.

4   Sort by type of clothing (long-sleeve blouses, short-sleeve blouses), and then hang according to color.

5   Take precautions to protect your clothing from moths. I store things that are really precious in breathable garment bags, and I use cedar-scented wood chips for everything else.

6   When it comes to shoes, I save dust bags for the most expensive—and sometimes even the boxes.

GUEST BEDROOM

WE HAD BIG AMBITIONS for our guest room: We wanted it to be as luxe and relaxing as the nicest hotel in town—until it's time to turn it into a nursery. So maybe it's not L'Ermitage Beverly Hills, but we really do roll out the red carpet in the hopes that guests have a great time and feel like our home is their home. And for us, this starts by making sure guests know that we've planned for their arrival and that we're not just begrudgingly shoving them in a room that happens to be clean.

THE GUEST ROOM BEDSIDE TABLE

Besides essentials like an iPhone plug, I also put out a tray to collect jewelry and watches, a water carafe and glasses, fresh flowers, a beautifully scented candle, a throw blanket during cooler months, and a handful of magazines—generally the more tabloidy the better. It's so important to me that guests feel like we really want them to be there, and I've found that these small touches make everyone feel extra welcome.

ESSENTIALS FOR BEING A TOURIST

Whenever you stay in a city with friends, you kind of want to be autonomous—particularly if you're staying for more than a day or two. To that end, we've assembled a tourist kit that we can roll out for any houseguests. It includes a map of the area (it's hard to get a sense of a place when you're looking on your phone); a list of great restaurants for breakfast, coffee, brunch, lunch, and dinner; our favorite stores; and any guest passes that we have to Los Angeles museums and cultural institutions. It's also nice to pick up a local listings magazine so that they can get a sense of what's going on in town.

RENTING

.... *1* ....

Make your bedroom pretty: Flowers on a weekly basis and really beautiful calming art are worthy splurges. It's so nice to wake up and see something gorgeous!

.... *2* ....

Likewise, invest in really great sheets—we spend a third of our lives in bed! Even if you eventually move into a bigger bed, you can always use nice sheets on a guest bed or pull-out!

.... *3* ....

If you have room at the end of the bed, get X-benches or poufs, so that you have a place to sit down and put on your shoes without crashing around the bedroom. Make a rule that it won't be a catch all for discarded clothes, as a cluttered bedroom is not a peaceful bedroom! These are the sort of pieces that you can easily use elsewhere when you move.

.... *4* ....

Get a super fluffy rug so that you have a nice and soft place to put your feet when you step out of bed.

.... *5* ....

Don't worry about having a nice nightstand—these are often covered up by a lamp or books anyway. Just be sure that it has some drawers so you can hide unsightlies.

.... *6* ....

Bedrooms generally need curtains for privacy, but don't invest in custom shades. Go for something that you can easily hem yourself (like the curtains at Ikea).

.... *7* ....

A great mattress is a key investment—it makes the biggest difference.

OWNING

1

Ditch the box spring and invest in an actual bed that has a nice headboard.

2

Splurge on custom curtains—and extra points for blackout shades.

3

Consider wall mounting your bedside lighting and sinking the cords in the wall in order to clear space and clutter from your bedside tables.

4

We don't have a dresser in our bedroom because our closet has tons of built-in storage—but if you do have one, make sure that it fits with the aesthetic and make it as pretty as possible. Often, flanking lamps and some trays to curate jewelry will do the trick.

5

Build out your closet: California Closet, the Container Store, and Ikea all have great options. You should maximize every inch so that you can shut the doors and have a clutter-free bedroom. This is also a good investment for the resale value of your home, as this is one of the first things that women in particular look at. People don't have a lot of imagination when they see an empty closet, but when they see plenty of hanging space and drawers they're thrilled!

6

Install good lighting in your closet and a full-size mirror.

7

A really beautiful pendant light can pull a bedroom together—get a chrome-dipped lightbulb though, so you're not staring up into a bright light. As in most rooms, putting the lights on a dimmer is essential.

chapter

////////////////////// 5 //////////////////////

BATH

//

round
brass
mirror

statement
wallpaper

funky
pendant

carrara
Top

unlaquered
brass
details

brass &
glass
sconce

brass
plumbing
fixtures

the importance of
DETAILS

/////////////////////////////

OH, BATHROOMS: While the smallness of the space is wonderfully manageable (you can really make it its own world), the functionality of a bathroom can be pretty limiting, which might be why you tend to see variations on either end of the spectrum: totally pristine and stunning, on the one hand, and so inherently ugly and unappealing that you want out as quickly as possible, on the other. I've had both. There are times—particularly with a rental—when there's little you can do to dress up cracked tiles and an aging toilet. You can get a new seat, you can add lots of pretty trappings to the counter, you can invest in a nice, enameled trash can and a luxe shower curtain—but if its soul is kind of ugly, that's hard to completely conceal.

Fortunately, now that we own a house, we got the chance to do up our bathrooms in a way we'd never been able to before. (Note: You never saw wide shots of my bathroom in our apartment, and this is precisely why.) It's a total luxury, but we have two and a half bathrooms. The guest bathroom is fine,

serviceable, nothing to write home about (and not something that we sank huge bucks into with our main round of remodeling and decoration), but we spent a lot of energy on our half-bathroom, which is a tiny space off the kitchen.

Fortunately, the master bath was already airy, light, and lined with nice finishings like white marble, so we had to do only a minimal amount to make it into a perfectly functioning space (it even has two sinks, which we've found to be one of the keys to a happy marriage). The light is flattering, the layout makes sense, and aside from needing some extra storage and little decorative moments, it was essentially complete.

When it comes to decorating, the key is "less is more," because, like a great kitchen, a great bathroom should put pride of place on really nice finishings and detail work, rather than a million design flourishes that eat up valuable counter space. For those things that are nice to have out, the same rule applies: Make it pretty.

guest bathroom essentials

//////////////////////////////////////

WE WENT NUTS in our powder room. I was so thrilled to have a small space in which to really go for it, as I've never had the guts to wallpaper an entire room before (at roughly fifteen square feet, this didn't seem that extreme). Amber convinced me to give this big floral print, designed by Ellie Cashman, a try—I had assumed it would be completely overwhelming—and I could not love it more: It's so dramatic, and so lush, and it makes me feel like I've stepped into a totally different world. In fact, the powder room just might be my favorite room in the house.

The bathroom definitely didn't always look this way. We inherited a room that was red and yellow with intricately beaded chandeliers, which definitely didn't fit with our general aesthetic. While it would have been pretty easy to let it slide and back-burner the space, we decided to jump in, and it's become this huge statement in our house, which goes to show that small spaces can be just as dramatic as giant rooms.

We had a professional install the wallpaper—this was definitely not something I felt comfortable doing on my own (as I've mentioned, I'm not that handy). In all, it was a bit of an investment (wallpaper is definitely more of a spend than paint) but so, so worth it.

pretty hand towel options

//////////////////////////////////////

FOR THE POWDER ROOM, which is what guests use when we have dinner parties, I keep a stash of paper hand towels in a stack by the sink, since there's something a little unappealing about using an already wet towel to dry your hands.

In the guest bathroom for overnight stays, I offer simple terry cloth towels, as that's what you actually want to use to wash your hands and face. Even though they look so pretty, I'm not into thin, overly-starched monogrammed linens, as they're not very absorbent, and you always feel like a jerk when you actually use them and mess up their perfection. I find that people feel more at home when you offer them things they actually feel comfortable using!

FINDING A SCENT FOR YOUR HOUSE

WHENEVER I GO TO MY parents' house in Northern California, the scent reinforces that I am home—it smells like pine and the ocean, and it will forever conjure up my childhood and the comfort of being with my mom and dad. Scent is a powerful thing, and something that I absolutely don't take lightly in the home I've created with G.

We don't just have one signature scent though—I change candles and hand soaps throughout the year to match the season. Maybe I'm sentimental, but I love to smell woodsier things when it's holiday time, and in the summer I gravitate toward lighter fragrances, like lemon and verbena. In an effort to make the scent profiles a little more complex, I don't buy candles that match hand soaps and lotions. Instead, I layer them, so the effect feels more sophisticated. I place a handful of candles throughout the house and nice hand soaps and lotions near all the sinks, both in the kitchen and all the bathrooms.

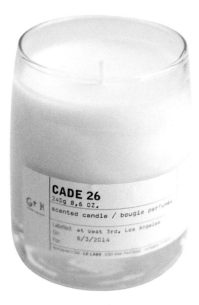

fall

winter

spring

summer

ART
alternatives

I LOVE THE IDEA of hanging a beautiful painting or photograph in a bathroom, though it's not always practical, particularly if your bathroom isn't well ventilated and you tend to steam up the space every time you take a shower.

To that end, I've come up with a handful of alternatives throughout the year for adding some color and interest to the space, without adding too many nonfunctional flourishes that eat up precious space. After all, bathrooms absolutely have to multitask. And there's a fine line between making it useful and making it pretty: You can't store your makeup in a hall closet, nor do you want a hairdryer and a million brushes permanently scattered over the counter. Here's how I use beauty products (which are often actually quite beautiful) to elevate the space.

1   Mount acrylic nail polish trays on the wall and arrange shades as an ombré or a rainbow.

2   Add a shelf to display beautiful perfume bottles that are both old and new—this is a great place to introduce some flea market finds in the mix.

3   Collect mini saucers and beautiful trays as catchalls for the counter and use them to create little vignettes. That collection of brushes looks much better when it's arranged on a mirrored tray or kept in a pretty jar.

4   Frame wallpaper. The glass will give it some extra-protection from the humidity, plus it's inherently not precious, so it's not the end of the world if you have to swap in a different sheet in a few years when it starts to look weathered. Along the same lines, consider stretching a beautiful canvas textile on a wooden frame.

room spray

fresh
flowers

brushes in old
candle jars

BA ES

diptyque 34 boulevard saint germain 34 boulevard saint germain parisse

parfum d'intérieur
interior scent

Dominique Ropion

FREDERIC MALLE

Petite Chérie
ANNICK GOUTAL

Fleurs
d'Orange
SERGE LUTENS

Tray to corral perfumes

essentials in apothecary jars

WHAT'S *on my* BATHROOM COUNTER

IF I USE SOMETHING EVERY DAY, I make sure that it's either on the counter or in the drawers closest to the counter. There's no sense in making the process of fetching everything to get ready in the morning a longer ordeal than the act itself.

So, I try to buy the most appealing versions of everyday things as possible, whether it's a Mason Pearson brush or an all-black hairdryer. And then I find pretty containers for everything that's itty-bitty, which is a huge upgrade over Q-tip packaging. Ultimately, when I burn down a candle in a pretty jar (from Diptyque, etc.), I save the jar for bathroom display. I also buy Mint Julep cups online, since they're the perfect height for storing makeup brushes and small bouquets of flowers.

BEDDING AND TOWELING are two categories where it's easy to spend a lot of money—and it's not always necessary. I think the quality of a great towel really comes down to absorbency, as there's nothing worse than wrapping yourself in a towel that just sort of moves water around your body. I also like the idea of using an organic cotton or bamboo, as those more basic, untreated fibers tend to be highly absorbent.

After sullying way too many white towels and turning them into foundation battlegrounds, I now invest in black hand towels for makeup removal. They are obviously much easier to keep clean!

In general, these are my go-to brands.

Coyuchi: I love that these are organic cotton—they're also very absorbant.

Williams-Sonoma Home: If you like monogramming and a more classic and tailored look, they have great options and a nice palette.

Company Store: They offer a veritable 64-pack of colors, including softer pastels. The prices here are really reasonable, too.

Abyss: Hyper-pigmented and super absorbant, I couldn't be a bigger fan of this toweling line. It's available at retailers like Bloomingdale's.

how to organize your makeup drawer

LIKE MOST OF THE GIRLS I know, I have a lot of makeup, yet I only wear about seven products religiously. Still, you never know when you're going to want purple eye shadow or a bright coral lip, so unless it's legitimately expired, or something that needs to be replaced quite frequently (mascara), I collect it in a storage system I've created to keep the more unique products out of the way.

HOW TO KEEP

a guest bathroom stocked

WE HAVE A SECOND FULL BATHROOM that's designated for guests, and in this space, we've really upped our toiletry game to ensure that it's as hotel-like as possible. I, personally, hate traveling with a full toiletry kit, or even a blow-dryer, so I make it a point to fill the cabinets with anything someone might need when they visit. When you're a guest, it's such a luxury and blessing to be able to find, say, a tampon, without having to ask for one. And the same goes for other key items such as Q-tips, stain remover, and Advil. Here's our list of what we keep perennially stocked.

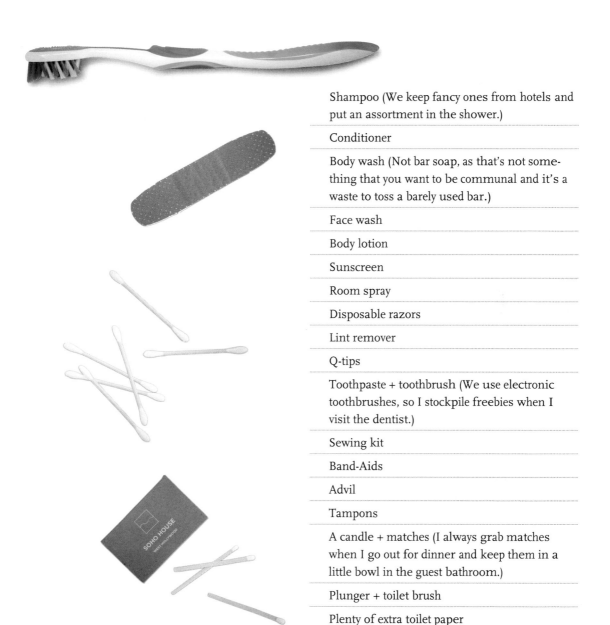

Shampoo (We keep fancy ones from hotels and put an assortment in the shower.)

Conditioner

Body wash (Not bar soap, as that's not something that you want to be communal and it's a waste to toss a barely used bar.)

Face wash

Body lotion

Sunscreen

Room spray

Disposable razors

Lint remover

Q-tips

Toothpaste + toothbrush (We use electronic toothbrushes, so I stockpile freebies when I visit the dentist.)

Sewing kit

Band-Aids

Advil

Tampons

A candle + matches (I always grab matches when I go out for dinner and keep them in a little bowl in the guest bathroom.)

Plunger + toilet brush

Plenty of extra toilet paper

RENTING

1

Go nuts on pretty storage containers and vessels, particularly if your bathroom counters have seen better days. If that's the case, consider layering a bigger lacquer tray over a nastier counter to house things like your toothbrush and makeup brushes.

2

Get some storage, like a leaning bookshelf, which you can fill with cute baskets. Be careful of storage that you put over the toilet!

3

Replace less-than-awesome knobs—even on the bathroom storage that you buy. (Just save the originals for when you move out.)

4

Find your signature scent: It's always good to have a candle or pretty room spray or diffuser.

5

Invest in pretty towels that you'd be happy to hang—they take up a lot of wall space.

6

Get a new toilet seat (or ask your landlord to swap the toilet seat for you). Enough said.

OWNING

1

Redo your counters, even if it's just re-grouting the tile—same for the shower. Grout can play host to mold and mildew.

2

Install water-saving showerheads—better for the environment and your budget.

3

Invest in perfect lighting—and new mirrors, particularly if yours aren't big enough to let you see the majority of your outfit.

4

Putting in a new faucet—if the bathroom warrants it—is actually really easy, and can make a big difference.

5

Recover the existing cabinets, or replace them if necessary: We painted them white and swapped the knobs. It gave the room an instant face-lift.

6

If we didn't have two sinks in our countertop, that's definitely something we would have considered investing in. It's a cliché but it's true—kind of a marriage saver!

chapter

////////////// 6 //////////////

HOME OFFICE

//

geometric
plant
holders

custom
acrylic
whiteboard

ladder
bookcases
flank
windows
to add a
library
vibe

white
drapes
add
warmth

agate
bookends

acrylic
accessories

colorful
rug

upholstered
corkboards in
black ticking
stripe

The importance of

ORGANIZATION

//////////////////////////////

GEOFFREY AND I WORK from our house, so we've made our third bedroom into a proper office—not proper in the sense that there are cubicles and a water cooler but in the sense that we have created a space where we can both spend our days getting stuff done. Without killing each other. Whether you have a home-based office or just need a station where you can get through the week's mail and write thank-you notes, everyone needs a space in their home where they can take care of things and file papers away.

The key, really, is to ensure that all of those papers don't get away from you. You don't want to find that you're burying things that are actually important under things that should have gone straight into the recycling bin. I've also had to train myself to repeatedly go through my stash of pens, paper clips, and the like so that I don't end up with a burgeoning junk drawer full of things that don't actually work (e.g., dried-up Bic pens).

It would be very easy to create stacks of paper in our office, if only because it's very easy to put mail, magazine tears, and printouts aside, either because you're going to deal with them later or because you think you might need something in the near-to-distant future. Corralling the chaos has really become all about dealing with everything in the moment, and then immediately shepherding it to its proper place, whether it's a clearly labeled folder in a filing cabinet or the trash.

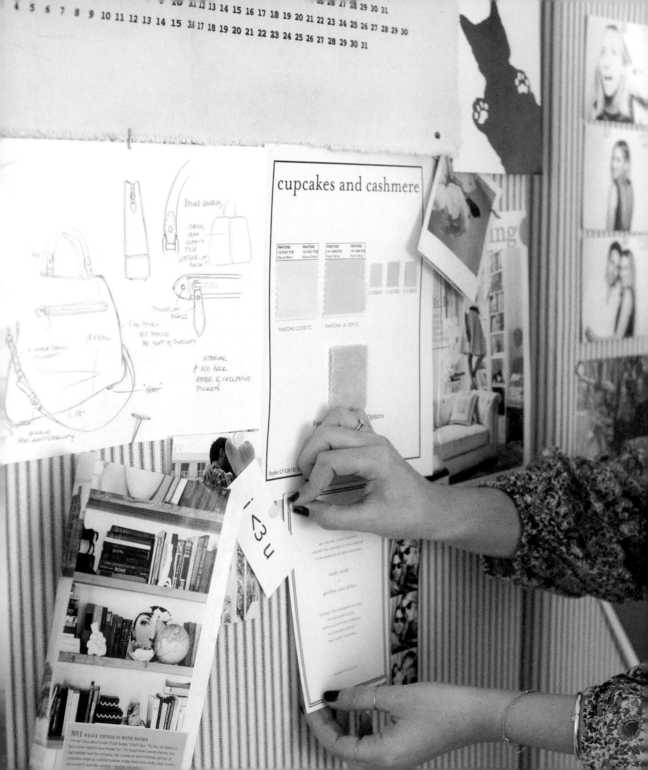

REINING IN THE CHAOS

moving past the whiteboard

NOTHING SAYS BLEH TO ME in an office like a whiteboard—sure, they're useful if you're doing major planning sessions or the like, but they just scream corporate. Plus, I've always found that if I write something down on a whiteboard, I end up having to either document it with my camera or rewrite it on a piece of paper. For our new office, we abandoned the whiteboard concept and opted for corkboards and plexiglass instead. I can write on the plexiglass with wet-erase markers (they require you to actually get a damp paper towel to get rid of what you've just written instead of everything just ending up on the back of your hand) and pin invitations and important lists to the corkboard. (You can get a piece of plexiglass from decentlyexposed.com, an Australian brand.) Both are actually aesthetically pleasing ways to store information, and looking at them helps me feel more creative and focused.

OFFICE
bookshelves

WE HAVE TWO LARGE, airy bookshelves in the corner of our office, and they're not really for books. Sure, they house a few things, but I primarily use them to store beauty products I intend to try, fun sculptural elements like a brass peace sign from Jayson Home, things I love (e.g., photos of me and G), and things I find inspirational, including some achievements over the years (like the bag I co-designed with Coach several years ago). I love being able to glance up from my laptop and see the history of the blog expressed on those simple shelves—it reminds me of what I've come from, what's important to me, everything that I've done, and why I love *Cupcakes & Cashmere* so much.

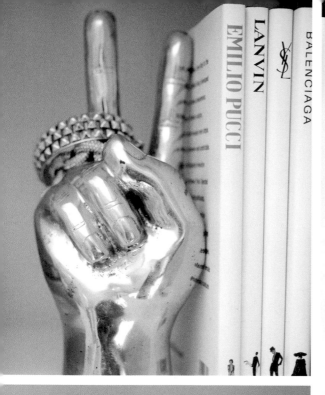

resources for
CUTE OFFICE SUPPLIES

I HAVE A PRETTY SIGNIFICANT—dare I say HUGE—soft spot for office supplies, to the point that you'll only find display-worthy pens in the house. I just can't write my to-do lists and notes (which I'm obsessive about) without a pen that I actually want to hold in my hand. I love Le Pen, Roller Ball, and Gelly Roll pens (yes, the kind you used as a kid).

While I keep my calendar electronically, I keep a physical desk calendar on display as well (I like to see the entire month in one sweep without having to switch windows on my computer), and I keep notes and to-do lists on my desk for easy accessibility. And while Post-its work fine, the to-do lists available at stores like Sugar Paper take a mundane element and make it beautiful (think: gold foil writing and pretty paper).

And I absolutely think it's worth investing in paper clips, binder clips, scissors, and so on that match your aesthetic—they can make the sometimes odious task of household chores much more appealing, plus there's no reason that something can't be both useful and pretty! Here are my favorite resources for stocking up on office supplies.

See Jane Work. They have tons of great boutique brands, from Rifle Paper Company to Portola.

Poppin. This cute resource does pop arty desk accessories in a range of colors, meaning that if you'd like it all to coordinate, this is definitely your place.

Anthropologie. While they're not known for office supplies, they do have great ones, whether it's pretty cups to co-opt for pencils or really gorgeous wall calendars, scissors, and mouse pads.

Russell + Hazel. I love their binders, simple notepads, and streamlined journals.

Muji. I can go to Muji for something simple like a clear acrylic tray and walk out with about twenty Technicolored pen markers, too.

Smythson. There's nothing more luxe than their leather journals. They're wonderfully flexible (stiff journals are difficult to write in, in my experience).

Schoolhouse Electric. This started as a lighting company, though they've branched out to other facets of the home, including the office. They sell a really nice range of supplies, from Postalco to Delfonics, plus they have wonderfully old-fashioned wire baskets and trash cans.

Notemaker. This Australian site offers an encyclopedia's worth of brands, including Lovely Pigeon (love their copper geometric notebooks), Life Stationery, Decomposition, and Studio Sarah.

essential elements for any organized drawer

AS I'VE DISCUSSED, if you don't stay on top of your supply drawer, it can quickly gremlinify and get completely out-of-hand, to the extent that you can never find what you need and you're flooded with everything that you don't. Maybe it's just me, but if there's too much in front of me, I can see nothing and will spend five minutes searching for a stapler that's right in front of my face.

I keep my desk drawers super organized (Lucite trays organize things in a way that doesn't scream corporate) and give each element its own place. That way, I know at a glance if I'm running low on stamps or envelopes, and whether I need to stock up on Post-its and pens.

bringing in the green

OFFICES CAN QUICKLY become clinical, particularly if the palette revolves around white and you're trying to keep clutter away. It was important to me that—just like in the rest of the house—we introduced splashes of color and that there be an element or two that is actually living, whether it's fresh flowers or a potted plant.

Since we don't have a ton of space—particularly on our work surfaces—I looked to introduce plants both on the floor and in the air. We placed a potted plant on the bookshelves and, of course, the dangling planters from the ceiling. Not only do these add a nice shot of green, but they lend extra texture to the room.

WINDOW

Treatments

WHEN AMBER SUGGESTED window treatments for our office, I was a little surprised—and definitely didn't think we needed them. After all, a pretty high hedge surrounds our house, and the windows of the office look out onto our backyard. It's also not overly sunny. But Amber insisted because she felt that it would do a ton to soften the space and add a bit more character—and she was totally right. In another brilliant twist, she hung them as close to the ceiling as possible, which creates the illusion of a much bigger space.

Custom window treatments and blinds can be ridiculously expensive, but there are tons of much more affordable options out there, particularly if you don't need curtains that will block out all the light and some noisy neighbors.

WINDOW TREATMENT RESOURCES

Ikea. These are great, simple, inexpensive, and easy to customize (they come extra long so you can trim them down and hem them with tape).

West Elm. Besides basic panels, they also offer really simple hardware that fits with any aesthetic.

Restoration Hardware. Custom shades are the standard here, and they are nice—with price tags to match. This is definitely a good option when you've bought a home and are looking for window treatments to last.

Crate and Barrel. Subtle prints and classic neutrals are mainstays here. Most are really straightforward and easy to install, and while they're definitely not cheap, they're a good choice if you're staying put for awhile.

Pottery Barn. This is a great resource for blackout roman shades, along with filmier curtains.

RENTING

.... *1* ....

Bring in some potted plants. It's so inspiring to look at fresh greenery.

.... *2* ....

If you're carving out a section of your living room to use as a home office, invest in sleek office supplies that are pretty enough to be out—that way, your desk doesn't turn into a distracting mess, reminding that you should be working rather than cocktailing.

.... *3* ....

I keep my desk super minimal: My computer, a chair, a light source—that way it's an appealing place to sit and I don't find myself wandering over to work on the couch. Boundaries are essential.

.... *4* ....

Put a blanket over your filing cabinet, or put it in a closet where you don't have to look at it everyday. If possible, put your printer on it in the closet—ensure that you can put work "away," so that you can unwind after hours.

.... *5* ....

Choose a desk with as small of a footprint as possible: Figure out exactly how much space you have and then don't choose anything that's bigger, as you'll fill it up if you have it.

.... *6* ....

If your office is in the living room, co-opt a dining room chair (so long as it's supportive enough) instead of investing in a big, bulky desk chair. If you have the luxury of a room on its own, then absolutely get a great chair that you'll have for years that will support your back.

.... *7* ....

To save space, consider a clip-on Tolomeo lamp or something similar, which you can install on a shelf above your desk (again, small footprint).

OWNING

1

Bring in bookshelves: Don't go for built-ins if there's a chance that your office will become, oh, I don't know—a nursery!

2

Do invest in permanent storage—drawers in a closet, etc.—so that you're not stuck with filing cabinets forever. You can always use these drawers for clothing instead, if the room changes functions.

3

I need something on which to keep myself organized, but, as mentioned, am not a big fan of whiteboards. Use corkboard or framed acrylic instead.

4

Take the time to organize your cords, as the same rules about hiding clutter apply.

5

Go for the right beautiful desk chair—it doesn't have to be synonymous with techy or clunky to support your back (eBay and Craigslist are great resources)

6

Add elements that aren't normally in an office, like a nice rug and curtains—you don't want it to feel like a sterile cubicle or a transient space. There should be inspirational things on the shelves as well, whether it's art, framed photos, or objects with special meaning.

7

Paint it a clean, neutral color that's not distracting.

8

I've made it a point to ensure that my desk is permanent: The power cord is hard to remove, I'm set up in an ergonomic way, etc. That way, it's very difficult for me to relocate my "office" to the living room couch or the dining room table. It keeps work in the office, and leaves the rest of the house to be a home.

9

Finally, I always have fresh flowers and a candle burning—it keeps the room light and inspiring.

WINE #1   WINE #2   WINE #3

chapter

COZY, LOW-KEY, CASUAL NIGHTS IN

In the past few years,
I've almost single-handedly
devoted myself to mastering
the art of midweek
entertaining.

IT CAN BE A BALLSY MOVE, particularly if you're cooking anything remotely involved, but I find that it's often easier to align everyone's busy schedules for a Tuesday or Wednesday get-together than a prized Saturday night (and for friends with little ones, it seems like a midweek babysitter is infinitely easier to come by than one on Friday).

What seems to work even better, particularly for those who are inclined to flake (you know who they are), is to rope your friends into an impromptu get-together day of. In fact, this is the sphere in which I operate with the most comfort, since sometimes you wake up in the morning and all you want is to play Scrabble and eat Pigs in a Blanket with some of your nearest and dearest. A few quick texts later, and you have something to look forward to without creating a scenario where you have tons of hours, or even days, to obsess about how the night might go . . . which sort of defeats the point of entertaining in the first place! I'm kind of convinced that spur-of-the-moment treats, thanks in no small part to the fact that there's no pressure, are always more fun. Everyone is always blown away and impressed by the most minimal effort.

In this chapter, we'll tackle just those scenarios—casual nights in, whether with a date or your closest girlfriends—where the evening revolves around something entertaining, a signature cocktail, a no-fuss app, and some great, potentially called-in food. If you haven't noticed, people these days tend to gravitate more to simple treats (mini grilled cheese sandwiches, tacos) than to a more elaborate meal. The major upside is that you can pull off an evening like this with minimal prep work, and almost even less time in the kitchen—meaning that you can spend a full day at the office, zip home, throw some things in a punch bowl, and have a great night in. Also, we live in an informal age—where it's often easiest to round people up by email or text so they can respond right away.

That said, if you have enough time, anything with a theme is pretty great to spin an invitation out of, making it a cute opportunity to send a piece of old-fashioned mail.

RETRO
GAME
NIGHT

Invite

For game night, I have two tricks up my sleeve. I've sourced vintage Scrabble pieces off eBay and then sent them out, spelling "Game Night" or my friend's first name, along with a cute note. You can also spell out a personalized invitation with Scrabble pieces, photograph it, and then send the picture as an invite. I've also scanned a playing card, blown it up to invite size, and used the white side to write out the details of the event.

Menu

Pigs in a Blanket

Chex Mix Redux

Old-school desserts:

	Ding Dongs
	Hostess Cupcakes
	Whoopie pies

Old Fashioneds

pigs in a blanket

These are worth making from scratch, as it's hard to find more gourmet versions in the frozen food section! They're also very easy, and the fact that you made an effort will impress guests.

Yield: Serves 4 to 6

Ingredients:

1 large egg

1 package frozen puff pastry, thawed

1 14-oz. package cocktail wieners

Variety of mustards

1 Preheat the oven to the temperature indicated on the puff pastry package.
2 In a small bowl, beat the egg and 2 to 3 table-spoons of water together to make an egg wash. Set aside.
3 Open the puff pastry flat on a cutting board and cut it into 2-inch (5-cm) squares.
4 Place a wiener in the corner of a square and roll it up in the puff pastry.
5 Brush the tip of the puff pastry lightly with egg wash and press it to the rolled wiener to secure the dough. Set seam-side down on a baking sheet and brush the top of the rolled wiener with egg wash.
6 Bake according to the puff pastry package instructions to ensure you get a nice golden-brown finish.
7 Serve with a variety of nice mustards.

chex mix redux

Adding a few other salty snacks to the Chex Mix takes it to the next level.

Yield: Serves a crowd

Ingredients:

2 bags Chex Mix Bold

1 bag Gardetto's

1 bag Bugles

1 bag Munchies Cheese Fix

Place all the snacks in a large bowl, mix together, and enjoy!

old-fashioned

Yield: Makes 1 cocktail

Ingredients:

1 ¼ teaspoons sugar (or 1 sugar cube)

2-3 dashes Angostura bitters

1 dash Angostura orange bitters

2 ½ ounces (75 ml) Rittenhouse Rye
  (or other American whiskey)

½ fresh orange wheel, for garnish

1 Place sugar, both bitters, and a splash of water
   in a lowball glass and muddle together, creating
   a light paste.

2 Add the rye and 1 or 2 large ice cubes. Stir to
   combine.

3 Drop in the orange wheel half to garnish.

Decor

This is the sort of evening that's best spent hud-
dling around a coffee table—if you have a fireplace,
get it roaring! Bring out a stack of extra blankets
and floor cushions, and pull the throw pillows
off the couch. This isn't a dinner party per se, as
there's no meal served—it's really just about light
noshing on great snacks and excellent drinks. The
trick is to ensure people are extra-comfortable, so
that they can settle down to play games for hours.
This isn't the sort of evening that should go down
with everyone perched precariously on bar stools
around the kitchen island. You want to be able to
kick off your shoes, recline, and play to win!

Games

| Balderdash |
| Bridge |
| Cards Against Humanity) *my favorite* |
| Gin rummy |
| Monopoly |
| Pictionary |
| Scrabble |
| Trivial Pursuit |

Attire

Encourage guests to wear retro-inspired outfits, whether that's a string of pearls, a full skirt, or pointy-toe pumps. Feel free to kick the heels off if you end up sitting on the floor!

)) Playlist

Dion and the Belmonts—"I Wonder Why"

The Elegants—"Little Star"

Frank Sinatra—"Luck Be a Lady"

Etta James—"At Last"

Sammy Davis Jr.—"What Can I Do"

Dean Martin—"Everybody Loves Somebody"

Nat King Cole—"Smile"

Bing Crosby—"Around the World"

Fred Astaire—"Cheek to Cheek"

Harry Connick Jr.—"Save the Last Dance for Me"

Bobby Darin—"Beyond the Sea"

Andy Williams—"Can't Take My Eyes off You"

Michael Bublé—"The Way You Look Tonight"

Frank Sinatra—"Fly Me to the Moon"

Elvis Presley—"Don't Be Cruel"

the bachelorette / the bachelor weekly viewing party

THIS IS A NIGHT THAT'S ABOUT INDULGING VICES, and all the many things that we might just be a little embarrassed to love. This is the night where you get to eat slightly naughty food and celebrate loving bad TV with your friends.

✉ INVITE 📑

No fancy invite required, just be sure that everyone rolls in at least half an hour before the show so they can get their drinks and settle into prime viewing position.

☰ MENU ☰

I'm always a big fan of theme-ing out, and making the takeout match the destination or hometown visit happening on the show. If they're on an exotic vacation in Bangkok, order Thai food; if they're visiting someone's parents in Fort Worth, order up the BBQ. Everyone needs to be at attention, in front of the TV, so this is not a night that you cook.

For dessert, Ring Pops are an obvious choice, plus all the classic movie candies like Junior Mints, Dots, Jujubes, Red Vines, and M&Ms. You can do a make-your-own-candy-stash bar, or simply put some bowls around the room.

🍸 DRINK 🍷

Again, this needs to be an easy serve-yourself scenario, so keep it simple and limit the choices to beer and wine. You can always pre-frost your beer mugs and add a slice of lemon or lime to dress them up.

▾▾▾ DECOR ▾▾▾

Red roses, candles.

⚞ ATTIRE ⚟

Anything casual and comfortable for a night spent in front of the TV.

⚘ ACTIVITY ⚘

You get extra points if you turn the show into a drinking game, based on the tics of the contestants. For example, every time someone says "true love" or "soul mate," drink. You can also set up a betting pool based on who is going to be eliminated. The loser is the next one to host.

blind wine tasting

THIS IS A LATE-AFTERNOON PARTY that can transition into evening (or a pot-luck)—it's like bringing wine country down to your house, without having to drive between vineyards.

First, choose whether you'll be tasting whites, rosés, reds, or champagnes, and then pick a region such as France, Napa, or Italy, and decide on a price—for example, nobody can spend more than $20. Depending on the number of guests, have everyone bring one or two bottles of their favorite wine that fits the criteria. When they arrive, put the bottles in paper bags, wrap twine around the top so you can't see the label, and number the bags. (Every bottle should be at the same temperature.) Then, get your guests munching on appetizers so they're not drinking on an empty stomach!

✉ INVITE 🖃

A quick invite scribbled onto the back of a paper coaster.

▤▤ MENU ▤

Whatever you're drinking will dictate the food:
If you're drinking rosé, serve a savory tart (like asparagus with gruyere).
If you're drinking champagne, serve oysters.
If you're drinking white, serve pita with hummus.
If you're drinking red, serve a cheese plate with charcuterie.

▽▽▽ DECOR ▽▽▽

Paper place mats with scorecards on them

♫♪♩ PLAYLIST ♫♪

The soundtrack from *Sideways*.

⌂ ATTIRE ✄

A dark shirt in case you spill on yourself!

ACTIVITY

Create a little scorecard of the qualities you're evaluating—I usually go for color, taste, and smell. As you taste each wine, give a rating for each one. At the end, whoever brought the wine that got the most votes wins a prize. The prize should be a gift certificate of the designated amount to a wine store. (Remind your guests that they don't have to finish every glass poured!)

chapter

8

MONTHLY DINNER PARTIES

a little more formal

Pulling together some Old-Fashioneds and Chex Mix on a Tuesday night is admittedly not that challenging.

I'M HERE TO ARGUE that upping the ante ever so slightly and doing a Tuesday night dinner party doesn't have to be that much more of a lift.

Ultimately, the same rules apply: Single friends are always looking for midweek activities, while married-with-children couples often can only find a willing babysitter during the week, meaning that you'll find a million willing and eager partners-in-crime. And any sort of enthusiasm goes a long way in making a night a success.

When it comes to the guest list for a great and successful dinner party, I always like it to be a mix of the known and unknown—couples I think might like each other, singles I think might like each other. With the latter, the key is to include an odd mix of singles (e.g., three), so that nobody feels as if they've been put on an awkward blind date with six other people as witnesses. Whenever possible, I like to separate spouses at the table so that they speak to people other than each other (you know how that goes), and make sure that there's an equal mix of sexes around the table. If I know I'm dealing with some friends who tend to be clingy (i.e., super averse to being separated), I'll place them side by side, and I use hand-drawn place cards to enforce the arrangement.

To minimize stress the day of, I try to keep the menu relatively laid-back and streamlined (people don't love overly fancy food, anyway, so no need

for major fireworks, particularly on a Monday or Tuesday). It's usually a signature cocktail; one appetizer plus something super simple like a bowl of nuts, hummus, or a cheese plate; a salad; and pasta or maybe a simple chicken with a starch and vegetable. Dessert can be luxe or it can be something laid-back, like a down-and-dirty build-your-own-sundae bar. I mean, who doesn't love a build-your-own-sundae bar?

I get as much out of the way in the morning as possible. I'll assemble any flowers (though this is worth doing the day before, if you can), set the table, make the salad dressing and put it in a jar in the fridge, pre-cut anything needed for the salad, wash and dry the lettuce, and chill some bottles of white wine or rosé.

After work, I light a candle, turn on the oven, and it's game on. But it's not stressful, particularly because so many of the things you forget to do until the last minute (setting the table) are already done. As always, the goal is to wrap things up in the kitchen (as much as possible) ten minutes before guests are scheduled to arrive so I can be barefoot with a glass of wine in hand by the time they stream through the door. The big upside of having an open kitchen with stools, though, is that if I'm putting some last-minute touches on a dish, guests can hang out with me while I cook.

CLASSIC
DINNER
PARTY

I LIKE TO DO PASTA for dinner parties, since it's easy to adjust the quantity without worrying about significant timing issues (e.g., doing a bigger roast). Plus, it's perfect for family-style serving and people are always happy to see it on the menu.

Invite

A simple email should suffice!

Menu

Cheese and charcuterie plate (people are often timid about diving into cheese, so I always put some dents in it before guests arrive)

Olives (make sure to put out a bowl for pits)

Linguini al'arrabiata

Caesar salad

Baguette (warmed in oven)

linguini al'arrabiata

Yield: Serves 4-6

Ingredients:

¹/₄ cup (60 ml) olive oil

1 yellow onion, chopped

3 cloves fresh garlic, finely chopped

3 tablespoons fresh thyme (or 1 tablespoon dried)

1 tablespoon red pepper flakes

2 28-oz (794-g) cans crushed tomatoes

1 tablespoon salt, plus more to taste

1 box linguini

Grated Parmesan, for garnish

Fresh basil, for garnish

1 Heat the oil in a large pot over medium-high heat. Add the onion and sauté for 5 to 7 minutes, or until soft.

2 Add the garlic and stir for 20 to 30 seconds, until it becomes fragrant. Add the thyme and red pepper and stir for 1 to 2 minutes.

3 Pour in the tomatoes and the salt, stirring to combine.

4 Reduce heat to low and simmer until the sauce is reduced by at least half (20 to 30 minutes). Taste and add more salt, if necessary.

5 Meanwhile, fill a large pot with water and bring to a boil. Cook the pasta according to package directions.

6 Drain the pasta, then place it back into the empty pot over medium heat. Add several ladles of the arrabiata sauce and cook until everything is combined.

7 Serve in large bowls with grated Parmesan and a chiffonade of basil.

caesar salad

Yield: Serves 4-6

Ingredients:

1 clove garlic, halved

4-5 anchovy fillets

Juice of 2 lemons

1 ½ tablespoons Dijon mustard (the spicier, the better)

1 large egg yolk

½ cup (120 ml) olive oil

½-1 cup (60-120 g) freshly grated Parmesan cheese

Salt and pepper, to taste

2-3 heads romaine lettuce, torn into pieces

Croutons

Parmesan cheese, for shaving

1   Take the halved garlic clove and rub the cut sides on the inside of your serving bowl, then discard.

2   In a blender, mix the anchovies, lemon juice, mustard, and egg yolk until well combined. With the blender still running, slowly pour in the olive oil. When done blending, pour the dressing into a bowl, mix in the Parmesan cheese, and season with salt and pepper. The dressing will keep for a couple of days in the refrigerator.

3   Pour 1–2 tablespoons of the dressing into the serving bowl and spread it around with the back of a spoon. Add the romaine lettuce and gently toss. Add more dressing, as desired, along with croutons, tossing to distribute evenly. Finish with shaved Parmesan and a sprinkling of salt.

Decor

Bust out your nicest china, but otherwise keep it simple. If you do flowers, they should be low, so people can easily converse across the table. I like to do place cards if it's eight or more, and I make it a point to separate spouses so that people are forced to mingle. Some couples really balk at this, but I think it's healthy to force them a little out of their comfort zone!

Playlist

Lucinda Williams—"Drunken Angel"

Coldplay—"Warning Sign" *my favorite*

Cowboy Junkies—"Misguided Angel"

Tracy Chapman—"Baby Can I Hold You"

Van Morrison—"Days Like This"

Dan Auerbach—"When the Night Comes"

Duffy—"Warwick Avenue"

Counting Crows—"Perfect Blue Buildings"

Amos Lee—"Baby I Want You"

Tom Petty—"Yer So Bad"

The Black Crowes—"She Talks to Angels"

Joe Purdy—"Waiting on Something Good"

Jackson Browne—"Doctor My Eyes"

Ed Harcourt—"She Fell into My Arms"

Amy Winehouse—"You Know I'm No Good"

I either go with bare feet or a pair of special, sparkly flats

Attire

Long, flowy dress, jeweled sandals, lots of bracelets (I love the sound they make when moving around), and a pretty, pastel lipstick.

take out night

OK, SO MAYBE IT SEEMS LIKE A COP OUT, but life gets busy, and that's no excuse not to see your friends! This is your last-minute dinner party go-to, when you find out a friend you've been dying to see is free, or you're too exhausted at the end of the day to pull off the culinary fireworks you promised your pals when you were feeling ambitious on Sunday. Plus, eating out can get expensive, and there's no substitute for being able to take your time around the dining room table. Just take a page out of *Mrs. Doubtfire*: Re-plate all the food and transfer sauces to little bowls. This is a night that's all about the company, but a few added touches can make it feel special and a little more considered.

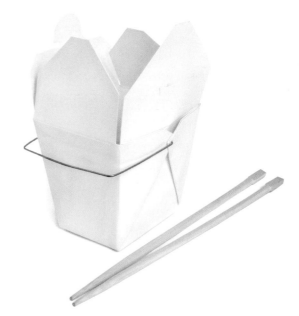

▤ MENU ▤

Chinese, Thai, Indian. Just pick one cuisine and order a bunch of different sides.

🍶 DRINK 🍷

Depending on your cuisine of choice, match the cocktails. If you order Japanese, for example, pick up some Kirin or sake. If you're having Chinese, a lychee martini works well, or a lassi if you're eating Indian food.

♫♪ PLAYLIST ♫♪

Fun, upbeat hip-hop or pop—think Beyoncé and Rihanna.

⚐ ATTIRE ⚐

What you wore to the office.

Taco bar

THIS IS EASY AND NO-FUSS, and while it's in a chapter about dinner parties, it actually works really well as a brunch, too. Just swap in eggs for the meat and add bacon and potatoes.

 INVITE

Choose a fiesta-style invite on Paperless Post—the site has great ones.

 MENU

Blackened grilled fish

Grilled steak

Grilled chicken

Tortillas (if there's a Mexican restaurant in the area, buy them there—go for the highest quality you can! Warm them in the oven or over the grill.)

Sour cream

Grated cheese

Guacamole

Salsa (some spicy, some not)

Chopped cilantro

Chopped onions

Lime wedges

Refried or black beans

DRINK

Micheladas: Salt the rim and combine Clamato with a beer like Pacifico or Sol, Tabasco, chili powder, and lime.

DECOR

Bust out the color! Do flowers in a more exotic shade than you normally would, like Gerbera daisies in fuchsia, bright green, or orange. Use a piece of oilcloth as a tablecloth and set out paper Mexican flags as decoration.

PLAYLIST

Buena Vista Social Club soundtrack.

ATTIRE

Anything bright and colorful.

chapter

///////////////////////// 9 /////////////////////////

DAY PARTIES

///

At least a few times
a year, I go all-out and
throw a daytime party.

THE CHALLENGE AND DELIGHT of a get-together when the sun is out is that every detail really counts and will absolutely be noticed, which makes the decor justify the effort . . . and also makes the event a bit more intimidating. Candlelight and lanterns are flattering for more than just faces.

The key to pulling it off is really in the prep work—and ensuring that you have an abundance of food and drink (honestly, people tend to have a great time unless they become keenly aware that they're hungry, thirsty, too hot, or too cold). And while I love everything to look as pretty as possible when the party kicks off, I always try to be a bit relaxed about it, since as soon as people start to dig in, it invariably becomes less "perfect." A party isn't fun if you spend its entire duration running around picking up abandoned glasses and crumpled napkins: At a certain point, you just have to let it go, so you don't spend the entire time working! If the budget permits and the party is big enough, it can be worth hiring a bartender to help serve drinks and clear empty glasses.

As for the prep part, it almost goes without saying that you should tackle as much as possible before the day of the event. A week or so before, after the invitations have gone out and the RSVPs

are collected, I sit down and work out the menu and quantity of food and drink needed. Then I make a checklist of all the to-dos, including a comprehensive grocery list and anything required for flowers and decor. Finally, I take all the tasks and put them into a checklist, marking what can be done days in advance and what needs to be taken care of within an hour of the party. Obviously, prep work includes cleaning the house, stocking the guest bathroom, running the dishwasher so your dishwasher is empty, and shopping.

The morning of, I get up a little earlier than normal and do a quick touch-up throughout the house before turning my attention to flowers and other bits of decor. Then I take care of anything else that I can knock off my list. Depending on the menu, this can range from assembling a punch to cutting up vegetables. And don't forget to take care of yourself! Hair, makeup, picking out an outfit—it can all create stress if you leave it to the thirty minutes before guests arrive, so at least think about what you'd like to wear in advance.

The most important splurge? Book a cleaning service for the day after, so you don't find yourself on your hands and knees mopping the floor when you may, or may not, have a hangover.

BAGEL
BRUNCH
&
MOVIES

THERE IS SOMETHING wonderfully indulgent about a morning spent in bed with the paper, some good TV, and a great cup of coffee. This is essentially that—but with all of your girlfriends, and on the couch. The breakfast spread should be something that can stay out all morning, so people can pick at it as they get hungry, and everyone should be able to eat out of their lap.

The main organizing principle, of course, is the movie selection. Pick something you all know by heart but don't get to watch that often, so you can tune in and out for your favorite parts. *Clueless, The Notebook, Pretty in Pink, Mean Girls, Sixteen Candles,* and *Pretty Woman* are all favorites with my friends.

Encourage friends to come over in comfy clothing—they don't need to wear their pajamas, but pajama bottoms wouldn't be such a bad choice! Provide extra socks or slippers and plenty of blankets.

place juice in small serving pitchers and ditch the cartons

Invite

Email—call it a pajama party during the day.

Menu

Bagels

Herbed cream cheese

Finely shaved red onion
($^{1}/_{4}$ inch [6 mm] thick or less)

Capers (drained and rinsed)

Smoked salmon

Lemon wedges

Tomato slices

Thinly sliced cucumber

herbed cream cheese

Yield: Makes about 2 cups (455 g)

Ingredients:

16 oz (455 g) cream cheese, at room temperature

8–10 sprigs fresh dill, chopped

6–10 fresh chives, chopped

1   In a large bowl, combine the cream cheese and
    herbs using either a fork or a hand mixer.
2   Transfer to a serving bowl.

Drink

Tangerine mimosas and grapefruit mimosas.

Attire

A Henley shirt and pajama pants.

baby shower

WHILE A TRADITIONAL AND FORMAL BABY SHOWER is always a nice way to go, it can be fun to shake things up and do things a bit differently. Keep in mind, for example, that it's often a disparate group of people who don't really know each other, so you can come up with lots of fun ways to break the ice that don't have to involve baby-food games or present unwrapping. As for the latter, ask the mom what she prefers—some people absolutely hate being the center of attention, while others want to open the gifts so everyone can see the cute baby stuff. Take the lead from the mom-to-be.

✉ INVITE ✉

This is an invitation that you'll want to design, print, and send with a proper RSVP (use an email address).

☰ MENU ☰

Grilled cheese bar (provide a variety of different combinations: mozzarella and tomato, ham and swiss, cheddar and apple chutney)
Ice cream sundae bar (the emphasis should be on old-fashioned toppings that we all remember from childhood)

🍸 DRINK 🍸

White wine and white wine spritzers. Also put out cranberry juice and lime for the mom-to-be to make her own mocktail.

▸▾▾ DECOR ▾▾◂

Again, take a cue from the mom-to-be here, though balloons, banners, a photo station, and children's books propped up are a fail-safe way to create a baby zone.

♫♩♪ PLAYLIST ♫♪♩

Hits from the year the mom-to-be was born.

👔 ATTIRE 👔

Simple dress.

👣 ACTIVITY 👣

You can play old-school games like guessing the baby food flavor, but it can be fun to do more craft-centric tasks to get people to bond. Some ideas are painting or tie-dyeing onesies, beading necklaces, painting book-plates for the baby's library, etc.

spa
day

THIS IS ABOUT PAMPERING, but not about over indulgence, so keep the menu light and simple.

✉ INVITE 🖃

Write the invitation out in lipstick (or just a part of it), photograph, and send. Tell your friends to wear flip-flops!

☰ MENU 🖃

Fruit kebabs
Cucumber and cream cheese finger sandwiches
Salad with grapefruit, toasted hazelnuts, and feta cheese
Crudités with tzatziki and hummus

🍸 DRINK 🍷

A pitcher of water with sliced cucumber and mint (do this ahead and let it steep in the fridge)—if you want to get fancy, freeze mint into ice cubes.

▽▽▽ DECOR ▽▽▽

Fill a bowl with single-use face masks and cucumber slices, and then set-up a mani/pedi station, complete with a bunch of nail polish color options and tools. Burn a candle with a scent that's extra-relaxing, like lavender.

♫♩♪ PLAYLIST ♫♩♪

Either female vocalists like Enya, classical, or nature sounds.

⌇ ATTIRE ⌇

Have guests arrive in their normal clothes, but encourage them to bring along a robe in case they want to change into it at some point.

👣 ACTIVITY 👣

This is all about nails and face self-care while spending some quality time with your friends. If budget allows, think about bringing in someone to do nails, or a hair person who can set up a braid bar. You could consider bringing in a makeup artist—tell your friends to bring their makeup bags, so they can learn how to apply the makeup they have.

🎁 FAVOR 🎁

Turn the occasion into a group gifting opportunity. Tell each guest to buy their favorite secret weapon beauty product (within a price suggestion/cap) and bring it wrapped. Then, everyone pulls a gift from the pool of presents—this way, you go home with something one of your friends thinks is awesome.

chapter

///////////////////// 10 /////////////////////

HOLIDAY PARTIES

///

I live for the holidays.

THERE ISN'T ONE that I don't wholeheartedly embrace and celebrate with a party. Presidents' Day? Awesome. St. Patrick's Day? Even better. Even the polarizing Valentine's Day—arguably the worst holiday for singles—was one of my favorite days of the year long before I met Geoffrey. I guess the point is that I don't really need much of an excuse to throw a party.

When I was growing up, my parents put a lot of effort into the big ones like Thanksgiving, Easter, and Christmas. Family and friends would gather, my parents would put out a huge spread, and games would often come out of the closet. And while the holidays themselves felt special—with my grandmother in the kitchen making latkes on Hanukkah or when I would head out the door to go trick-or-treating on Halloween—it was always the preparations beforehand that I loved the most.

Whether it was picking out my pumpkin for the perfect jack-o'-lantern in the middle of October or stringing up heart lights for Valentine's Day, those are the memories I treasure.

While I've held onto many of the traditions from my childhood, it's also been fun to create new ones for Geoffrey and me. We throw an annual "Friends-giving" each year a week or two before Thanksgiving just for friends. It's low-key, casual, and always ends with a semi-buzzed version of Pictionary or charades. Having things to look forward to throughout the year, whether centered around holidays or not, is what life is all about.

Like any big get-together, as corny and cliché as it sounds, what goes on the table—from the food to the flowers—is really only as important as who is around it. So here's to new traditions and great friends and family to celebrate them with.

VALENTINE'S
DAY PARTY

THIS GIRLS-ONLY PARTY is about celebrating the kind of love that always lasts! One of those rare occasions when you can go full-on girly, let your pink freak flag fly here and make everything pretty. Really, you can use appropriately hued candy as your primary point of decoration, whether bowls of pink M&Ms or rock candy arranged in pretty cocktail glasses.

Invite

An old-school Valentine with conversation hearts in the envelope.

Menu

Sparkly sugar cookies

Valentine's Day–themed marshmallows

Candy galore

Cookies & cream cake

Drink

Sparkling rosé or champagne (sugar the rims of the glasses with pink sugar).

Playlist

Ray LaMontagne—"Shelter"

Joni Mitchell—"A Case of You"

The Rolling Stones—"Wild Horses"

Van Morrison—"Crazy Love"

Norah Jones—"Turn Me On"

Mindy Smith—"One Moment More"

The Beatles—"Real Love"

Eric Clapton—"Wonderful Tonight"

Amos Lee—"Colors"

Grace Potter & the Nocturnals—"Falling or Flying"

Mazzy Star—"Fade into You" *my song with g!*

Dayna Manning—"I Want"

Ryan Adams—"Two"

Griffin House—"Only Love Remains"

Elliott Smith—"Miss Misery"

Decor

The pink amplifies the message, but there should be flowers on the scene, too. Lately, I've been loving ombré-ing my arrangements.

Attire

This is your chance to bring out your frilliest skirt with pink heels—feel free to bust out anything pink or remotely heart-shaped, too.

hydrangea ombré

THIS IS A REALLY **dramatic** floral arrangement that looks a lot more complicated than it really is. By using long, low vases filled with flowers in gradient colors, it has the ability to completely transform a space.

Materials:
Flowers in gradient colors (hydrangeas are my go-to)
Ti leaves
One or more long, low vases (I buy plastic ones at the Flower Mart)
Foam
Scissors

1 Trim the flowers so they're all the same height and arrange by color on the counter.
2 Cut the ti leaves so that they fit inside the vases (they're used to conceal the foam inside).
3 Place the foam blocks in the vases and fill with water.
4 Starting with the lightest color, place the flowers in the foam, adding more until a gradient is achieved.

light to dark

ugly sweater party

GEOFFREY AND I ALWAYS TRY to pull off a holiday party, and to mix things up a bit we usually ask our friends to bust out their ugliest sweater, which pretty much sets the tone. Weirdly, the sweaters tend to be awesome icebreakers, meaning the night goes off without a hitch (and a lot of new friendships are forged).

MENU

Hearty potato-leek soup (bonus points if you serve it in hollowed-out bread bowls)

Toasted open-face cheese sandwiches

Roasted chestnuts

Peppermint bark

Truffles

DRINK

Mulled wine, spiked eggnog, and apple cider.

DECOR

Hang mistletoe and twinkling star lights, and embrace a palette of dark jewel tones. Burn pine-scented or cedar-scented candles (anything woodsy is great), and use branches to make centerpieces. I also like to fill mint julep cup vases with cranberry branches (think beyond poinsettias). If you want to make a bigger centerpiece, set out a clear vase with cranberries on the bottom and white flowers on top.

PLAYLIST

Holiday music, of course!

ATTIRE

You don't want to be totally atrocious, so pair your ugly sweater with skinny black pants and jeweled flats.

friendsgiving

DON'T GET ME WRONG, I love to spend time with my parents, and I can't wait to establish even more traditions with my growing family, but I really, really love to do a Friendsgiving. It's so nice to sit over a very long and leisurely meal with good friends and have a bunch of laughs (and a lot of turkey)—it is always a pretty eclectic crew, with anyone who doesn't have plans on and around Thanksgiving, so it's different every year.

✉ INVITE 🗐

I like to send a proper card to make it into a real event—but that doesn't mean that it has to be formal.

▤ MENU 🗐

Turkey

Stuffing

Mashed potatoes (elevate them with Parmesan or truffle salt)

Roasted brussels sprouts or creamed spinach

Dinner rolls

Cranberry sauce

Gravy

Pumpkin pie

Pecan pie

Apple pie

Whipped cream!

◦◯◦ DRINK ☖☖

Citrus gin punch.

▾▿▾ DECOR ▾▿▾

I like to go pretty and festive by way of rustic with a gilded edge. I use a lot of natural elements to bring the outdoors in: a burlap runner, pine cones dipped in gold, and a low sculptural centerpiece dotted with smaller flower arrangements.

♫♩♩ PLAYLIST ♫♫♩

Motown—fun hits from the fifties and sixties.

⌒ ATTIRE ◞◞

Something really comfortable, like stretchy pants or a loose dress.

▲▵ FAVOR ▲▵

To-go boxes with leftovers.

chapter

11

OUTDOOR PARTIES

Oh, the pleasures of
entertaining outside.

FOR ONE, THERE'S NO KITCHEN TO CLEAN; for two, you get to leave the decorating to nature (more or less).

While living in Los Angeles means that I can head outdoors with a picnic basket pretty much all year round (I know, I know), there's still something about using the summer months for this style of entertaining that appeals to me.

With our new house, we also managed to acquire a small backyard, with a dinner party–appropriate table (we've made it look even bigger by hanging a mirror alongside one edge).

There's not a lot better than dining in candlelight underneath the stars. We also take advantage of

L.A.'s preferred form of entertainment—picnicking at the Hollywood Bowl— or taking in a movie at Hollywood Forever Cemetery (yes, it's a cemetery) to master the art of the picnic.

Whether you're spreading out a blanket in your own backyard or at the park down the street, dining alfresco can be a wonderfully laid-back affair that still presents the perfect opportunity to add some really fun design touches, like wax paper and twine–wrapped sandwiches, pickles in Weck jars, handheld desserts like homemade cupcakes and brownies, and champagne in plastic Govino glasses. Just because it's portable doesn't mean it can't be special!

CRAWFISH
BOIL

I LOVE NEW ORLEANS—and everything that goes with it. While I have yet to master the perfect beignet, I do love putting on a crawfish boil every summer. It's such a great opportunity to get a little messy and eat with your hands (it's also perfect for the Fourth of July).

Invite

Confetti in the envelope makes it extra festive.

Menu

Crawfish

Corn on the cob

Spicy mayo

King cake

Pralines

Had this in New Orleans and fell in love.

Drink

Abita beer

crawfish boil

Yield: 10 pounds (4.5 kg) of crawfish
(enough for 10–12 people)

Ingredients:

1/2 cup (120 g) kosher salt

3 tablespoons garlic powder

3 tablespoons Old Bay Seasoning

2 tablespoons onion powder

2 tablespoons dried thyme

5 bay leaves

3 pounds (1.4 kg) red potatoes

10 ears corn, halved

10 pounds (4.5 kg) crawfish, boiled and seasoned

Spicy mayo (mayo and a dash of hot sauce)

1 In a large stock pot, bring 6 gallons (23 L) of water, the salt, and the spices to a boil.

2 Add the potatoes and corn, cover, and cook for 12 to 15 minutes.

3 Add the crawfish and cook for 2 to 3 minutes, until heated through.

4 Carefully pour the boil through a large colander, or remove from pot with a chinois and place into a large bowl.

5 Place newspaper over a cloth-covered table, and pour the potatoes, corn, and crawfish across the surface.

6 Serve with spicy mayo.

Decor

This is a super-casual, eat-with-your-hands type of affair. Put newspaper down everywhere (it's messy), and make sure you have plenty of napkins and hot towels or wet wipes for people's hands.

Favor

Mardi Gras beads for people to wear.

Attire

Cut-offs, T-shirt, festive necklace, and tennis shoes. Also, a hat if you're out in the sun.

Playlist

Rebirth Brass Band—"Do Watcha Wanna"

Dr. John—"Iko Iko"

The Meters—"Cissy Strut"

Kermit Ruffins—"Drop Me Off in New Orleans"

Trombone Shorty—"Hurricane Season"

Louis Armstrong—"West End Blues"

Fats Domino—"Blueberry Hill"

Lee Dorsey—"Working in the Coal Mine"

Lake City Stompers—"Basin Street Blues"

Professor Longhair—"Go to the Mardi Gras"

Eddie Bo—"Tee Na Na Na Na Nay"

Trombone Shorty—"Suburbia"

Eddie Condon—"Chicago"

casual hat, statement necklace

outdoor screening

GEOFFREY AND I LOOKED into hosting an outdoor movie night with friends, and we were surprised that it's not that expensive to rent a screen and projector—we're dying to host an outdoor screening party in our backyard next summer.

📽 MENU 🎞

Truffled popcorn

Caramel or kettle corn

Chicken wings

Fancy nachos (melted real cheese with jalapeños, cilantro, black beans, sour cream)

Frozen treats (freeze Butterfinger Bites, Junior Mints, bonbons)

🍸 DRINK 🍸

Margaritas (make a big pitcher ahead of time).

▾▾▾ DECOR ▾▾▾

Bring out plenty of blankets and pillows—have friends bring extras if they can. Also, put out some beach chairs for people who can't sit on the ground for the duration of a movie. If you have one, or can find one to rent, a space heater is a good option.

👔 ATTIRE 👠👠

Wear layers and a cozy sweater—maybe even yoga pants. You are going to be sitting on the ground, after all, so you may as well be comfortable!

🎞 ACTIVITY 🎬

Choose an old-school summer classic, like *Grease*, *Jaws*, or *Dirty Dancing*.

resources

For those curious about the items featured in the book, I created a resources section so that you can see where everything is from, broken down by room.

LIVING ROOM
Leather couch—Restoration Hardware
Side tables—West Elm
Coffee table—West Elm
Green chairs—Crate and Barrel
Lamps—Haus Interiors
Framed photo—Gray Malin
Rug—Etsy, We Make Rugs
Fireplace lighting fixture—Schoolhouse Electric
Antelope bust—vintage
Pink neon tray—Alexandra Von Furstenberg
Pillows—Amber Interiors

ENTRYWAY
Console table—HD Buttercup
Mirror—vintage
Acrylic chair—eBay

TV ROOM
Sectional sofa—custom
Throw pillows—Amber Interiors
Rug—West Elm
Photographs—Max Wanger

DINING ROOM
Dining table—custom
Chairs—vintage
Bar cart—vintage
Chandelier—HD Buttercup

KITCHEN
Stools—Organic Modernism
Rug—Amber Interiors
Knobs and pulls—Home Depot
Faucets—Plumbers Surplus

MASTER BEDROOM
Bed—Room & Board
Bedding—Bed, Bath & Beyond
Chandelier—Shades of Light
Rug—Rugs USA
Pillows and Moroccan blanket—Amber Interiors
Nightstands—West Elm
Lamps—custom
Bench—custom

GUEST BEDROOM
Bed—Target
Shams and duvet—Biscuit Home
Coverlet—Restoration Hardware
Nightstands—Target
Sconces—Serena & Lily
Chandelier—Shades of Light
Blue pillow—Amber Interiors

POWDER ROOM
Wallpaper—Ellie Cashman
Sink—Restoration Hardware
Mirror—CB2
Pendant—Schoolhouse Electric
Sconce—Schoolhouse Electric

HOME OFFICE
Desk—West Elm
Chair—Zuo
Bookshelves—CB2
Rug—Lulu & Georgia
Bulletin board—Custom
Planters – Kelly Lamb
File cabinet—CB2
Console—Room & Board
Peace sign sculpture—Jayson Home

acknowledgments

I WOULD LIKE TO THANK my husband, Geoffrey, for his patience, for his unwavering support, and for still calling me his "bride." And for building a beautiful home with me that's filled with love, cute cats, and his famous chicken wings.

To my mom and dad, who have always taken an interest in things that matter to me and for never missing a blog post, even the first ones that were painful to read. As we prepare for the arrival of our first child, I can only hope to be half the parents that you've been to me.

To Elise for making the process of writing this book such a pleasure, especially with meetings that revolved around large quantities of dessert.

To Phoebe for working tirelessly by my side and for investing so much of your time and energy into bringing each page to life. And to Diana for being the organized voice of reason each time a particular task would seem too daunting.

To Amber, who helped make our home such a beautiful, inspiring place. But beyond your abilities as a great interior designer, it's our friendship that I treasure most.

To my editor, Rebecca (who gave birth while I wrote both my first and second books), for your guidance and enthusiasm. And to Laura, who has graciously stepped in both times she's been away and made me feel well taken care of.

To Ryan for being the first person to believe I should write a book, and to Cait for helping make this second one happen. And my appreciation goes out to Jenny for translating my requests into tastefully designed pages.

And finally to my wonderful readers for sharing my excitement about the little things in life and making my job so enjoyable. I can't thank you enough for your support and encouragement.

image credits

Photographs by Emily Schuman and Phoebe Dean, except for page 122 © Michela Ravasio / Stocksy United, pages 128–129 (letter tiles) ©iStock.com/asbe, page 129 (necklace) ©iStock.com/MarkSwallow, page 130 ©iStock.com/ranasu, page 131 ©iStock.com/assalve, page 134 ©iStock.com/happyfoto, page 139 ©iStock.com/lleerogers, page 142 ©iStock.com/chictype, page 143 ©iStock.com/Suzifoo, page 146 ©iStock.com/ermingut, page 152 ©iStock.com/pepifoto, page 153 ©iStock.com/subjug, pages 156–157 ©iStock.com/severija, page 161 (candy) ©iStock.com/IngaNielsen, page 164 ©iStock.com/deliormanli, page 165 ©iStock.com/PIKSEL, pages 168–169 ©iStock.com/A-S-L, page 171 (beads) ©iStock.com/Kathryn8, page 174 ©iStock.com/duckycards, page 175 ©iStock.com/amriphoto

THE TRIAL OF JESUS

THE
TRIAL OF JESUS

THE HON. JAMES C. McRUER

CHIEF JUSTICE OF THE HIGH COURT OF JUSTICE FOR ONTARIO

CLARKE, IRWIN & COMPANY LIMITED

TORONTO   1964   VANCOUVER

This book is dedicated to Mary — my wife

FOREWORD

CICERO HAS written that the greatest praise is to be praised by a praised man—*laudari a laudato viro.* Such was my personal feeling of having been praised when asked to write this Foreword. It is, therefore, in this spirit of deep gratitude and appreciation that I am genuinely honoured to write this Foreword for my esteemed friend, the Honourable J. C. McRuer, Chief Justice of the High Court for Ontario.

I read *The Trial of Jesus* with great and growing interest and I can single out only a few of the many reasons for praise and admiration. Never have I seen the evidence of injustice in the trial of Jesus so well collated and united, and the cumulative effect of violation after violation of injustice and illegality is most profound. And yet with all this, there is the keenest sense of complete objectivity and historical impartiality. The whole orderly and balanced presentation is harmoniously structured in the mores and culture of the times, and the depth of historical and religious background learning never distracts from nor diminishes the author's palpable respect and deep reverence for the Person of Jesus.

Our distinguished author in this book prescinds completely—and quite properly so—from our individual and collective guilt in the death of Jesus. He writes solely from the legal aspect and in so doing exhibits his great range of reading, his research and erudition, and the juridical excellence that has earned him a prominent place in the roster of Canadian jurists. This book will enhance his present premier position in legal scholarship, and we warmly recommend it and wish it the wide reading public it so richly deserves.

J. ELLIOTT MacGUIGAN, S. J.

Regis College
February 1964

PREFACE

THE OBJECT of this book is to relate the written account of the trial of Jesus, together with the relevant events which preceded it, to the political and religious affairs of his time as well as to what we know about the legal procedures of his day. The turbulent events of that period produced religious leaders with distorted minds just as similar events have done throughout history—leaders who departed widely from the true concepts of their faith to use the offices they held to serve unworthy ends. It may well be that those with whom we are concerned pursued their misguided course just as many Christians holding high ecclesiastical and civil offices have since done, sincerely believing that the end was a righteous one and the means justified.

The record as contained in the four Gospels is accepted as fact. Where the authors are at variance with one another, their differences are considered just as those found in the evidence of honest witnesses. All evidence is affected by the capacity of the witness to observe, his powers of accurate recollection, his gift of expression and, where his evidence depends on the word of others, the accuracy of the information communicated to him. It is for Biblical scholars to debate the authenticity of the Gospel records and how far one version of the same event is to be preferred to another. The approach of the layman is to accept what he finds and in doing so to treat the respective accounts as supplementing one another. This I have done.

I wish to acknowledge all the kindly assistance and encouragement that I have received from my friends in the accumulation of material for this little book. My particular thanks are due to the Right Reverend F. H. Wilkinson, M.A., D.D., Bishop of Toronto; Reverend E. Marshall Howse, D.D., pastor of Bloor Street United Church, Toronto; Canon Edward Every, M.A., St. George's Cathedral, Jerusalem, Jordan; the Reverend Father Elliott MacGuigan of Regis College, Toronto; and Rabbi Stuart E. Rosenberg of Beth Tzedec Congregation, Toronto. To these acknowledgments I gratefully add my warmest appreciation of all the kindness extended to me by the Editor and Staff of Clarke, Irwin & Co. Ltd.

J. C. McRuer

Osgoode Hall
February 1964

THE TRIAL OF JESUS

I

THURSDAY, a very sacred day of the Passover week, had almost passed. The Passover supper had been eaten, and at midnight the temple gates were thrown open.[1] Jesus, with eleven of his disciples, crossed the Kidron to the foot of the Mount of Olives—to the Garden of Gethsemane—there to practise his evening devotions; this he had done each night that week before he made his way up the hill to Bethany.

As he was engaged in prayer, through the gate in the city wall just across the valley there came a motley throng. The Levitical police from the temple led the way. With them were servants of the chief priests and the elders; Malchus, the high priest's slave, was there. This was no ordinary band of night adventurers. There were among them persons of rank and power: a group of chief priests and elders. All were accompanied by a small detachment of Roman soldiers. A strange assembly to be at large on the most sacred night of the most sacred week of the year to all Jewish people!

The moon was full. The little band in the garden could not help seeing the black mass approaching. Soon they would recognize none other than the treasurer of Jesus' disciples leading the multitude. Soon they would know the purpose of it all—to arrest Jesus of Nazareth.

II

IT IS ONLY against the background of the historical events that have converged to bring it about that any great political or religious trial can be examined. The trial of Jesus is no exception. Since the dawn of recorded time the political history of the Jewish people has been turbulent, but it probably never was more so than during the early part of the century that preceded the rise of the Star of Bethlehem.

Book after book of the Old Testament catalogues wars of conquest and wars of devastation and destruction. Jews were killed and massacred by the thousands and tens of thousands, and by the thousands and tens of thousands they were carried away into slavery. It was not until the rise of the Maccabees in the second century B.C. that the land of the Jews, Judea, really became a state of any consequence.

The Maccabean Wars expanded the boundaries of tiny Judea until they were comparable with those of the days of David and Solomon, and at the edge of the sword the boundaries of the Jewish religion were likewise expanded. The method was simple. Those who did not accept Judaism were destroyed. Ruthless as this form of conversion may appear, it is not to be forgotten that the political life and the religious life of the Jewish people were indistinguishable. Their God was a mighty God of war, defending his own and destroying their enemies. The result was that Judaism was re-established in the traditional homeland of King David, and it was raised to a power that even the Roman emperors could not disregard.

With the Roman intervention in 63 B.C. came not only political strife but civil war. The Jews were divided among themselves. Jewish leaders joined with the Romans against their

4

neighbours and then against their fellow Jews. At that time, the ruling class, headed by the Maccabean high priest Hyrcanus, compromised with the Romans.[1] Although the gates of Jerusalem were opened to Pompey, Aristobulus, a brother of Hyrcanus, defended the temple and the city with his intrepid followers at the cost of a thousand lives. Jerusalem was conquered and the temple fell. With its fall the resisting Jews were taught a Roman lesson: twelve thousand were massacred.[2] Judea was dismembered. It was not until the rise of Herod, called "the Great" by the Gentiles and by the Jews, "the Bloody," that the bitter and lethal struggle ceased to rage between the Romans and their Jewish supporters on the one side and the Jewish revolutionaries on the other.

Herod the Great became Governor of Galilee when only fifteen years of age.[3] He was an Edomite—one of a race of traditional enemies of the Jews. Herod was destined to dominate the political and religious affairs of the Jewish people for more than a quarter of a century before the birth of Jesus, while at the same time establishing a means of co-existence with their Roman masters. The means of co-existence adopted was a legacy from his father—flattery, bribery and ruthlessness. It made Herod king, but under him the Jewish people were to become little more than slaves. The Sanhedrin, the highest court of the Jewish people and their chief legislative body, was stripped of its real power and reduced to an ecclesiastical body dealing only with minor religious matters. The office of high priest was changed from a hereditary one of great dignity and authority to a servile piece of patronage at the disposal of Herod and his Roman masters. High priests were appointed and deposed in rapid succession. They were able to pay well for their appointments; the fruits of the offices were abundant.

5

The Jewish people hated Herod with a bitter hatred because he was an Edomite and also because he was a minion of Rome. This hatred mattered little to Herod as long as he bathed in the sunshine of Roman good will and held the power of taxation over the Jews, which he exploited to unbearable limits. He built and rebuilt great cities, and flattered Roman emperors with the names he gave to them. A magnificent palace was built at Caesarea on the Mediterranean coast to accommodate the Roman governor. Another of similar magnificence was built in Jerusalem to house the governor and his staff when he came from Caesarea to visit Jerusalem. As a mark of flattery to Mark Antony, the palace was called the Antonia. Not only did the Antonia serve as a residence for the Roman governor, it served as a citadel as well to house the authority and arms of Rome. It was built dominating the temple and the temple area, just as the temple dominated Jerusalem. To the Antonia we shall return.

On the site that is now known as the Citadel in Jerusalem Herod built for himself a magnificent palace. It was here that his son Antipas met Jesus face to face. Jericho was rebuilt in extravagant style two miles south of the Jericho of the Old Testament. Here Herod built two palaces, one called after Augustus and the other after Agrippa. The water resources of a parched country were conserved and developed. Aqueducts were built to supply water to Jerusalem, and springs were developed to provide water for Herod's palaces in Jericho and for agricultural expansion in that district. Fortresses were repaired and new ones built. In true Roman style, Jericho was provided with an amphitheatre and a hippodrome.

All this extravagance and luxury was repulsive to the Jews. It went against their traditions and violated their religious convictions. To placate them and assure himself some measure of

6

security, Herod rebuilt the temple in Jerusalem. To the Jews the temple was more than the heart of their national life: it was the most sacred place in the world. Only here could sacrifices be offered to the one God, Jehovah. A city of great palaces with a shrine to Jehovah in ruins was a city for which the Jews could have no respect. Although Herod could never hope to enjoy the confidence of the Jews, he could hope to appease their animosity by restoring their sacred shrine to something of the glory of the temple of Solomon. This he did. When completed, the building was a fitting rival of other great religious shrines of the world, whether in Athens or in Rome.

Concessions to the religious life of the Jews did not serve their purpose. The resentment they bore toward their political oppressors remained unabated. Many of their religious leaders were quite content to endure oppression with patience as they awaited a righteous redeemer who would come to deliver them. There were others less patient, such as the Zealots, who were ready to bring about their redemption by abrupt and violent means. Throughout the political life of Herodian Israel, if rebellion was not erupting, it was seething just below the surface; and wherever rebellion was seething, there the Zealots were. Nowhere were the political waters more turbulent than in Galilee.

The troubled life of Herod, although called "the Great," came to an end in the most abject misery. It was a life abounding in ruthlessness, crime, vain gratification of personal ambition and the degradation of the people over whom he ruled with the delegated power of Rome. As Herod's life was drawing to a close, he left Jerusalem for Jericho to spend his remaining few days. Two of the most revered Rabbis among the Jewish people, Judas and Matthias,[4] believing that Herod was dead, put themselves at the head of a gallant and reckless band

7

that determined to wipe away all traces of Herodian idolatry. The first move was to attack and destroy the golden eagle—the symbol of Rome—that hung over the gate of the temple. The two leaders and forty of their followers were seized by Herod's guards and taken to Jericho, there to be subjected to trial in the Roman theatre. With his fatal illness on him, Herod was carried on a couch to preside as judge and prosecutor. On his order the little band of rebels were all burned alive.[5] But this was not all. As his end approached, Herod realized that there would be joy in all Israel when the news of his death broke. He made up his mind that this should not be so. Calling together many of the leaders of Israel, he imprisoned them in the Hippodrome at Jericho with orders to his sister Salome that on his death all of them were to be slain, so that the joy of Israel would be turned to mourning. Salome wisely did not carry out her brother's orders.

Just five days before his death Herod had his last wish gratified. Augustus gave him permission to execute one of his sons, Antipater, who had been named in two wills to succeed his father as King of Judea.[6] While on his deathbed, Herod made a fourth will by which sons of his fourth wife, Malthake, a Samaritan, were the objects of his bounty. Archelaus was appointed King of Judea, and Antipas, Tetrarch of Galilee and Perea. Philip, a son by Cleopatra of Jerusalem, was made Tetrarch of the territory east of the Jordan. Herod may in fact have had the power to appoint his successor, but with shrewd prudence he made his appointments subject to the approval of Augustus.[7]

With the blood of tens of thousands of subject Jews on his hands and the destruction of his second wife Mariamne and three of his sons on his conscience, the old king died. It was into this distraught Herodian Jewish world that Jesus was born.

Herod's body was hardly in the grave before the ever-smouldering insurrection broke into flame. Resentment burned in the hearts of the Jewish people over the slaughter of their beloved Rabbis, Judas and Matthias. At the feast of the Passover, when the temple and its precincts were filled with worshippers, pilgrims prayed and talked sedition. Archelaus, the unconfirmed king, became uneasy. If rebellion broke out, Augustus would be disinclined to ratify Herod's will. So he decided to nip insurrection in the bud, and sent one thousand soldiers to the temple. The soldiers were assaulted and stoned. Unwilling to engage in open battle, the troops and their captain ran away. Archelaus replied with an army that attacked both those in the temple and the pilgrims to the Passover who dwelt in tents outside the temple area. Three thousand Jews were killed.[8]

Archelaus' troubles were not confined to his Jewish subjects. He was not to be confirmed in his kingdom without a struggle from another quarter. He became involved in a lawsuit as the defendant in what is probably the earliest recorded will case, and he found himself before no less a judge than Augustus Caesar. Antipas, who had been named King of Judea in his father's third will, attacked the will which named Archelaus and disputed his brother's right to be King of Judea. Archelaus and Antipas both set out for Rome, each taking with him an orator to speak in support of their respective cases and a whole retinue of relations to give evidence.

The case for Antipas was heard first. A cousin, Antipater, who was "a very subtle orator," spoke for him. His case was based on two grounds: first, Archelaus should not now be confirmed in the kingdom because he had assumed to act as king without first being confirmed in the office by Caesar; secondly, Herod was "in a dying condition of body and mind" when he named Archelaus king. The case for Antipas at first seemed a strong one. Archelaus had certainly assumed to act as king without Caesar's ratification. He had ordered many Jews to be destroyed as they came together for the Passover.[9] It was contended with great force that if there was to be punishment meted out, it should have been reserved for those having authority to impose it. In assuming to act as king, he "did injury to Caesar by usurping that authority." It was also charged that he changed commanders in the army and sat in judgment to determine lawsuits. The contention on this branch of the case was that Archelaus had proved that he could not be trusted with the authority of Caesar. The argument based on mental incapacity was not a convincing one to those who knew old Herod. Nor was it any credit to Archelaus. It was contended that, since Archelaus had been guilty of such slaughter while he pretended to be king, his father must not have been in sound mind when he made his will because "he knew his dispositions." In addition, Archelaus was also charged with having been disrespectful to his father by merry meeting "the very night in which he died," and "pretending to shed tears for him in the day time, like an actor on the stage."[10] Antipas then called many witnesses to support his charges against Archelaus, among whom were some of Archelaus' own relations, who had deserted him after having been brought to Rome to support his case.

The case for Antipas closed, Nicolaus, the orator engaged by Archelaus, replied with masterful skill. One by one he turned the accusations made against Archelaus to his own profit. The slaughter of the Jews on the feast day was not ordered under the pretence of exercising the power of Caesar, but its purpose was to suppress a revolution against the authority of Caesar. In a speech pungent with flattery he argued that Archelaus' superior fitness for the office was proof of the soundness of Herod's mind when he preferred him to Antipas to be king.[11] His concluding sentence was an argument hard for Caesar to reject:

> Caesar will not therefore disannul the testament of a man whom he had entirely supported, of his friend and confederate, and that which is committed to him in trust to ratify; nor will Caesar's virtuous and upright disposition, which is known and uncontested through all the habitable world, imitate the wickedness of these men in condemning a king as a madman, and as having lost his reason, while he hath bequeathed the succession to a good son of his, and to one who flies to Caesar's upright determination for refuge. Nor can Herod at any time have been mistaken in his judgment about a successor, while he showed so much prudence as to submit all to Caesar's determination.[12]

Caesar reserved judgment and later confirmed the will with some modifications; the kingdom of Herod the Great was divided into three. One-third went to Archelaus with the title of ethnarch and the promise of the title of king if he should prove himself worthy. To Antipas went Galilee and Perea with the title of tetrarch; and the remainder to a brother, Philip.[13] It could hardly be said that Caesar was a strictly disinterested judge when he sat in judgment to determine the testamentary capacity of old Herod. Under the will Caesar received "ten millions (of drachmae) of coined money, besides both vessels of gold and silver," and his wife, Julia, received "garments exceeding costly."[14] It is said, however, that the emperor kept only a few works of art for himself, and distributed the wealth left to him among the members of the Herodian family.[15]

Archelaus' rule in Judea was a short and unhappy one. He surpassed his father in cruelty and oppression. While he was still in Rome appearing before Caesar to support his father's will, rebellion broke out afresh in Judea. Varus, the Governor of Syria, was sent to quell the rebellion. He did so with ruthless punishment and returned to Syria, leaving Sabinius in charge. Sabinius provoked the Jews to further revolt. So great was their hatred of him that they were able to enlist the support of many of Herod's soldiers in their cause. On the feast of the Pentecost tens of thousands of men including many Galileans, Idumeans, and pilgrims from Jericho and beyond the Jordan so placed themselves in the city as to encircle the Romans. A fierce and bloody struggle ensued. The Jews fought with great courage, but armed as they were with slings and stones, the Romans dispersed and destroyed them with ease. Sabinius himself raided the temple treasury and stole 400 talents.[16] Sabinius won this battle but did not quell the revolt, which spread throughout Judea. Herodian palaces were attacked and burned. Some Herodian soldiers stood by the Romans and some deserted to the rebels. Local government of the Jewish people by Jews for all practical purposes virtually came to an end. Of the period Josephus says:

> And now Judea was full of robberies; and as the several companies of the seditious lighted upon any one to head them, he was created a king immediately, in order to do mischief to the public. They were in some small measure indeed, and in small matters, hurtful to the Romans; but the murders they committed upon their own people lasted a long while.[17]

Nowhere was the spirit of revolt more rampant than in Jesus' own province, Galilee. When Varus returned from Syria to suppress the rebellion, he caused two thousand men to be crucified. Their leaders he sent to Rome to be tried and punished.[18]

Archelaus was no match for the task of ruling such a turbulent people. He was weak, ruthless and self-indulgent. Like Antipas he fell into difficulties with irregular and unlawful marital alliances: he married his brother's wife. With money extracted from an impoverished people, he gratified his vanity with great palaces. The Jews and Samaritans, despite their mutual enmity, united to protest to Augustus Caesar who summoned Archelaus to Rome. There he was deposed, banished to Vienna in Gaul (Vienne, France) and had all his property confiscated.[19]

The banishment of Archelaus brought to an end the era of Jewish kings. The effective government of the Jewish people came under the Roman Procurator (governor), who for his comfort maintained his permanent residence at Caesarea and for the control of his subjects, a Roman army in barracks at the Antonia in Jerusalem. Here Roman sentinels kept watch over the temple. On great feast days the governor himself took direct charge, lest any disturbance should develop.

The powers of Jewish civil authorities were circumscribed. Judges were permitted to function in property cases but only to a limited extent in criminal cases. Roman customs, dues and taxes were collected by a detested class of Roman agents—the publicans. They sucked the blood of a subject people to satisfy the appetites of their masters. These officials were frequently changed by Tiberius. He likened them to flies on a sore. Those already sated with blood do not suck so hard as newcomers.[20]

The right to appoint the high priest, which had been assumed by Herod the Great, was now taken over by the Roman Procurator. The high priest's robes were put under a Roman guard at the Antonia. To the Jews this was not only a humiliation but a sacrilege. Three successive procurators during Jesus' lifetime failed to do more than keep rebellion among the Jews under control.

All these turbulent political events must have been discussed from day to day in Nazareth as Jesus worked at his carpenter's bench.

III

IN THE SYNAGOGUES of Galilee Jesus' voice was heard as one with a mission. "For I tell you, unless your righteousness exceeds that of the scribes and Pharisees, you will never enter the kingdom of heaven"[1] were strong words, revolutionary words, revolutionary words that preached rebellion not against the power of Rome but against special privilege in everything religious. He was a humble man, a carpenter's son. To the crowds that came to hear him he taught as a man of astonishing knowledge and as one who had authority—not as their scribes.

Such teaching could not long be disregarded by the religious rulers. It can hardly be mere coincidence that from these early days of his career the local scribes, Pharisees and Sadducees in Galilee were quick to seek anything in Jesus' teaching or behaviour that could be interpreted as unlawful. They were equally quick to lay snares for him in order to secure admissions that might support evidence of a capital crime.

The scribes were at the apex of the pyramid of honour in the Jewish religion at this time. They were not members of a religious party, but they held a religious status of ancient origin. It has been said that Babylon may have been the birthplace of their order, but be that as it may, they were to be found wherever there were Jews. A scribe was ordained by the laying on of hands and was addressed as "My great one" and "Master" or "Rabbi." Where the scribe walked the people respectfully gave way. According to tradition his religious status destined him for a place of great honour in the future world. The scribe was honoured by God himself and his praises sung by the angels. In Heaven would he hold the same offices of rank and distinction as on earth?

As a teacher or doctor of law,[2] the scribe was the final authority on all questions of law and sat as a judge in the Sanhedrin. Respected for his knowledge and as a man of peerless learning, he walked among the people as "the divine aristocrat among the vulgar herd of rude and profane 'country' people who 'know not the law' and are 'cursed.' "[3]

> Among their fellow men they were absolutely believed even if they were to declare that to be at the right hand which was at the left, or vice versa.[4]

Apart from the scribes, there were four main religious parties, or sects, among the Jews, all of which looked forward to the coming of the Messiah to deliver them out of bondage: the Zealots, the Pharisees, the Sadducees and the Essenes. Of these the Zealots were the most violent. They were always ready to hasten the coming of the Messiah by militant action. The Pharisees, who held the greatest representation among the people, were less contentious than the Zealots, but were by no means believers in non-resistance. Although they believed in the coming of the Messiah as a political and spiritual ideal, they did not advocate such force as might beget disaster. The Sadducees were much more sophisticated than either the Zealots or the Pharisees. They were prepared to enjoy any temporal power that their religion might give them without permitting this enjoyment to become politically embarrassing. The Essenes were a mystical sect, many of whom lived a monastic life upon which much light has been thrown by the discovery of the Dead Sea Scrolls at Qumran. They believed in living a life of social equality, purity, righteousness and perfect worship.[5]

Of these four sects we are concerned only with the Pharisees and Sadducees. Both these sects were of comparatively recent origin. Josephus places their beginnings about 150 B.C. It may well be that they were of more ancient origin and that it was only with the rise of the Maccabees that their orders took the form in which they were found during Jesus' lifetime. Josephus, himself a Pharisee, says of them: "A cunning sect they were, and soon elevated to a pitch of open fighting and doing mischief."[6] They disliked kings and refused to take the oath of allegiance to Caesar, for which they were fined. Because they foretold the destruction of Herod's kingdom their leaders were put to death.

At the time of Christ the Pharisaical "fraternity" was comparatively small. It numbered about 6,000 members, but it was nevertheless very influential. The object of the Pharisaic association was to maintain strict obedience to the whole body of Levitical law, and to pay punctiliously their tithes and religious dues. Pharisaism was a sort of inner circle of Jews that demanded of its members implicit obedience to Jewish law. Notwithstanding their exclusiveness, in Herodian and Roman times this sect was the dominating element in the religious affairs of the Jewish people.[7] According to their direction the people performed their divine worship, prayers and sacrifices.[8] All this gave them a special claim on the promises of the law and made for them an association that, according to them, represented the true Israel. Contact with non-Pharisees was avoided wherever possible. All others were unclean.[9]

They were the legal scholars. Not only did they declare the written law but they developed the oral law of the scribes. Josephus tells us, ". . . the Pharisees have delivered to the people a great many observances by succession from their fathers, which are not written in the laws of Moses; . . ."[10] It was the voice of the Pharisees that was heard on behalf of the people, whether it was before the high priest or the king.[11]

There was as wide a division between the Pharisees and the Sadducees as there was between them and many of the most learned scribes, who not only refused to associate with them but held them in contempt.[12] To many the word "Pharisee" was then, as it is today, synonymous with the word "hypocrite." Josephus says they were a sect of the Jews "who valued themselves highly upon the exact skill they had in the law of their fathers, and made men believe they were highly favoured by God. . . ."[13] They believed in the immortality of the soul of the righteous, while the wicked were punished by eternal torment.[14]

The Sadducees were not a fraternity or inner circle, but were a hereditary and ancient priestly class. They constituted the nobility of the Jewish people and thus we find many high priests coming from the Sadducean party.[15] Annas was a Sadducee.[16] However, all priests were not Sadducees. Many Pharisaic leaders were priests, and Pharisees generally recognized and acknowledged the privileges of the priesthood.[17]

In matters of theological doctrine, the Pharisees were in

17

open conflict with the Sadducees, with whom they struggled for both civil and ecclesiastical power. Free will, predestination and the resurrection of the body were all areas of dogmatic differences.[18] The Sadducees believed that the souls of men died with their bodies. They did not believe in the resurrection of the body nor retribution in a future life. Neither did they believe in predestination, but "that good and evil are the choice of man who can do one or the other at his discretion" and consequently that God exercises "no influence upon human actions, and that man is therefore himself the cause of his own prosperity and adversity."[19]

In addition to the doctrinal differences between the Sadducees and Pharisees over the immortality of the soul, there was a fundamental difference over what constituted the law of the Jews. The Sadducees acknowledged only the written Torah as binding and rejected the entire traditional interpretation as well as the further development that the law had undergone during the course of centuries at the hands of the scribes.[20] It is not unfair to say that the Sadducees were really more concerned with the political power that their ecclesiastical offices gave them than with the spiritual affairs of the people. To make themselves secure in this power during the Herodian-Roman period, it was necessary for them to accommodate their views to those of the Pharisees.[21] But the differences between these two sects concerning the interpretation of the law and ceremonial practices gave rise to perpetual controversy.[22]

Whatever may have been the theological and philosophical differences between the Pharisees and the Sadducees, Jesus' early ministry arrested the attention of the leaders of both parties. They saw in his teaching new concepts of human values and human obligations—concepts that, if allowed to take root and grow, would destroy not only much of the power they

18

wielded in religious affairs, but many of the vested interests which were the source of their great wealth. From the early days they were united in one thing—the determination that Jesus' ministry should be of short duration.

IV

THE PHARISEES soon found legal precedents for their first accusation. Profaning the Sabbath was a capital offence for which the offender was liable to be condemned to execution by stoning.[1] None other than Moses had sentenced a man to death for gathering sticks on the Sabbath.[2] As Jesus passed through the grain fields, his disciples picked ears of grain to satisfy their hunger.[3] When the Pharisees saw it, they said to him: "Look, your disciples are doing what is not lawful to do on the Sabbath." Jesus replied with a knowledge of this law that was more than a match for his accusers. Had not David satisfied his hunger with holy bread?[4] Did not the priests in the earliest days profane the Sabbath and remain blameless?[5] He carried his case into the synagogue where he challenged his accusers: "Is it lawful on the sabbath to do good or to do harm, to save life or to kill?" And he healed a man with a withered hand. The Jewish law provided that "the saving of human life sets aside the laws of the sabbath," but what it did not permit was healing where there was no risk of immediate death.[6] The man with the withered hand was not one who was dangerously ill. Jesus had replied not only with words but deeds. To the Pharisees all this was religious sedition, but they promptly directed themselves to deal with it as civil sedition.

They silently left the synagogue and "immediately held counsel with the Herodians against him, how to destroy him."[7]

The Herodians were not a religious sect but a political party of Galilee who were more involved with conflicting secular loyalties than any matters of doctrine.[8] The union of the Pharisees and Herodians of Galilee in a common objective was to bear fruit in Jerusalem during Jesus' last days there.

Jesus went his way throughout all Galilee preaching, and where his voice was heard the people were astonished. "Where did this man get this wisdom. . .?"[9] It is of no small significance that Herod Antipas, with blood on his hands and guilt on his conscience, took Jesus to be John the Baptist raised from the dead.[10]

The events in Galilee could not escape the attention of the highest Jewish ecclesiastical authorities. Very soon a deputation of scribes and Pharisees was dispatched from Jerusalem to interrogate Jesus. The first attack was based on a hygienic tradition that had almost the force of law. "Why do your disciples transgress the tradition of the elders? For they do not wash their hands when they eat."[11] Here Jesus joined issue with his critics and took the offensive. From then until the day of his death there was to be no compromise. What mattered was not man-made doctrines but the things of the spirit:

> You hypocrites! Well did Isaiah prophesy of you, when he said:
>> 'This people honors me with their lips,
>> but their heart is far from me;
>> in vain do they worship me,
>> teaching as doctrines the precepts of men.' [12]

And with words that were to echo down the corridors of time in the face of his accusers, he called the people together and said: "Hear and understand: not what goes into the mouth defiles a man, but what comes out of the mouth, this defiles a man."[13]

It is not surprising that the Pharisaic delegation did not take kindly to such forthright criticism with all its implications. The disciples warned Jesus: "Do you know that the Pharisees were offended when they heard this saying?"[14] But, undeterred, Jesus pressed the attack: "Every plant which my heavenly Father has not planted will be rooted up. Let them alone; they are blind guides. And if a blind man leads a blind man, both will fall into a pit."[15] To Peter Jesus made doubly clear what his answer was to the charge that he had broken the Jewish law:

> Do you not see that whatever goes into the mouth passes into the stomach, and so passes on? But what comes out of the mouth proceeds from the heart, and this defiles a man. For out of the heart come evil thoughts, murder, adultery, fornication, theft, false witness, slander. These are what defile a man; but to eat with unwashed hands does not defile a man.[16]

This engagement over, Jesus pursued his ministry of teaching and healing. It mattered not whether it was on the Mediterranean at Tyre and Sidon, in Canaan or on the shores of the Sea of Galilee. Wherever he went the multitudes followed him, and what appeared to the ecclesiastical authorities to be seeds of religious revolution continued to be sown. The Pharisees and Sadducees now pooled their strategic resources to suppress the germination of any revolutionary ideas.

The plan laid was not new. From the days of Socrates it was followed wherever civil or ecclesiastical authorities sought to use the judicial process to terminate a life that was disturbing their interests. Accordingly, questions were put to Jesus that were designed to bring forth incriminating answers that would serve their purposes. "Show us a sign from Heaven"[17] was a legalistic trap involving the offences of sorcery and false prophecy. Each was punishable by death,[18] the former by stoning[19] and the latter by strangulation.[20] But Jesus did not fall into this trap. His reply neither placated his questioners nor served their purposes:

> You know how to interpret the appearance of the sky, but you cannot interpret the signs of the times. An evil and adulterous generation seeks for a sign, but no sign shall be given to it except the sign of Jonah.[21]

In due course it became clear that Jesus could not accomplish his mission without meeting face to face those who held the reins of priestly power. They had laid their plans and he had laid his. He well knew they were determined that he should die. He was determined that the spiritual life of mankind should be freed from the corrupt and corrosive ecclesiastical bonds which were strangling its growth and expression. So he "began to show his disciples that he must go to Jerusalem" where he would "suffer many things from the elders and chief priests and scribes, and be killed, . . ." [22] Calling the twelve together he said to them: "Behold, we are going up to Jerusalem, and everything that is written of the Son of man by the prophets will be accomplished." [23] To Jerusalem he went— to the temple, to Annas, to Caiaphas, to Pilate and to Calvary.

The most direct route from Galilee to Jerusalem lay through the hills of Samaria. Jesus would have taken this route had it not been that his messengers who had been sent ahead reported back to him that no Jew going to Jerusalem was safe at the hands of the Samaritans. The alternative way led through the Decapolis beyond the Jordan, a region populated more by Gentiles than Jews. The way lay by the scene of Jesus' baptism in the Jordan and through Jericho some fifty miles south of the Sea of Galilee. Some months were spent en route, teaching and healing. The Jordan was ultimately crossed at a place sacred to the memory of all Jews—the place where Joshua led the children of Israel into the Promised Land.

Wherever Jesus went he was followed by crowds of spiritually hungry people. Wherever the crowds were, there too were the Pharisaic vigilantes—vigilantes who were astute to seize every opportunity not only to embarrass and discredit Jesus with his followers but to catch him in heretical teaching. The ageless problem of divorce appeared to be a subject that was peculiarly suited to that purpose. The question was a simple one to ask but a difficult one to answer. The books of Moses did not agree. "Is it lawful to divorce one's wife for any cause?"[24] Jesus based his answer on the earliest authority, which gave to marriage something more than a mere civil concept— something in the nature of a spiritual alliance. "Have you not read that he who made them from the beginning made them male and female, and said 'For this reason a man shall leave his father and mother and be joined to his wife, and the two shall become one?' So they are no longer two but one. What therefore God has joined together, let no man put asunder." [25] His inquisitors pressed their case by confronting him with the Mosaic law taken from Deuteronomy which permitted a man to divorce his wife by merely giving her a certificate of divorce.[26] Jesus' reply was simple: it was not so "from the beginning"; the only justification for divorce was unchastity. The Pharisaic emissaries neither discredited Jesus nor made out any case of heresy against him. Jesus went on with his teaching.

During that last fortnight Jesus was only one of thousands of pilgrims converging on Jerusalem from every direction

23

to celebrate the feast most sacred to all Jews—the feast of the Passover. To this feast came Jews who spoke the language of every country touched by civilization, there to mingle with Jews of the neighbouring Hebrew world. At no time were the shadows of religious corruption more boldly etched on all that was sacred to devout Jews than at the feast of the Passover.

As Jesus and his little band approached Jericho, they saw there an oasis in a parched countryside, an oasis made luxuriant by flowing springs of fresh water. Over 4,000 years before Moses looked out from Mount Nebo over the city of palm trees, Jericho had been a paleolithic settlement. When Joshua laid seige to it, it was the oldest known inhabited city in the world. But the Jericho of Christ was not the Jericho of Joshua. As Jesus entered it, the city was one of the most modern in the East,[27] throbbing with commerce and basking in the sunshine of royal patronage. True, the ravages of war and earthquakes had repeatedly destroyed all but traces of what had gone before, but it had always been rebuilt, though not precisely on the same site. The Jericho Jesus entered was the Jericho that Antony had given to Cleopatra as a solace for not making her Queen of Judea. She rented the rich gardens to Herod the Great for a princely sum and Herod rebuilt the city in keeping with the rent he was required to pay. There he built for himself a palace, there he made his winter home and there he died.

It was in this garden city that Jesus was to spend his last Sabbath on earth. He was to spend it with a man who was not only rich but one who was despised by the Hebrews—a Hebrew in the employ of the Roman government as its chief tax-gatherer. Throughout human history tax-gatherers have not enjoyed much popularity, but tax-gatherers for foreign powers of occupation have always been loathed with a loathing reserved for traitors.

Zacchaeus, the chief tax-gatherer at Jericho, was a small man but a determined one. He had a burning desire to see and hear Jesus, but Jesus' followers would not permit him to come near their teacher. Discarding the dignity of his office, Zacchaeus resorted to the simple expedient of a small boy—he climbed a sycamore tree. This probably caused no small stir among those who knew the tax-gatherer, and it did not pass unnoticed by Jesus. Zacchaeus was invited to play host to the man he was so curious to see. Little did he realize who his guest really was. Jesus' invitation to "make haste and come down; for I must stay at your house today" raised a discordant murmur in the crowd. The friend of the humble, the poor and the destitute had invited himself to be entertained by a man exacting Roman tribute from his fellow Hebrews. The murmur soon became an outburst of dissent: "He has gone in to be the guest of a man who is a sinner." [28] Zacchaeus may have been a tax-gatherer but he was a just one. The accusations made against him stirred him to his own defence. While the Mosaic law required only tithing, Zacchaeus gave half his goods to the poor. Moreover, if he defrauded anyone he restored it fourfold,[29] even though the law required him only to make restitution and add one-fifth.[30]

What passed between Zacchaeus and Jesus on that last Sabbath is locked up in unrecorded history—nor do we know what became of Zacchaeus. Tradition has it that he was ordained Bishop of Caesarea by Peter much against his will.[31] Whatever became of the little man in the tree, the events of that day demonstrated for eternity that Jesus was the friend of the penitent rich and the penitent poor alike.

With the Sabbath over, Zacchaeus' hospitality ended, and Jesus commenced the steep climb from Jericho to Jerusalem. This road was to become the scene of one of his simplest but most penetrating parables, the parable of the good Samaritan. He had travelled this old Roman road before. It leads through a bleak and lonely wilderness populated by Bedouin nomads. The hills are barren and the gorges are deep. It was in a cave just off this road that, according to tradition, Elijah made his retreat by the brook Cherith.[32] Rising some 3,500 feet in less than 20 miles, the road passes through the villages of Bethany and Bethpage.

As Jesus approached these villages he travelled as an outlaw. The Sanhedrin at Jerusalem had put a price on his head, but the time was not ripe for his arrest. He had a very great following that could not be disregarded, and evidence against him to support a charge punishable by death was frail indeed. The Jewish leaders were in a very real dilemma. The Roman governor had the final word in any matter involving the sentence of death. It was quite unlikely that Rome would be much interested in matters having to do with a man who had created some religious strife among the Jews. It would be better to have no prosecution than a prosecution that failed. As the chief priests and ruling Pharisees gathered in solemn council, they asked themselves a simple but penetrating question: "What are we to do? . . . If we let him go on thus, every one will believe in him, and the Romans will come and destroy both our holy place and our nation."[33] In this, one sees an element of propaganda. Propaganda for political purposes is no modern invention. Just why the Romans would destroy the temple and the nation because Jesus had a great following of believers is difficult to imagine, but the declaration served a convenient purpose: to link Jesus and his followers with the Roman menace. Caiaphas, the high priest, was quick to seize the opportunity and make full use of the instrument that was in his hand. The nation must be saved from Roman destruction, so he declared, ". . . it is expedient for you that one man should die for the people, and that the whole nation should not perish." [34] With that declaration the council of the court of justice was converted into a conspirators' den: ". . . from that day on they took counsel how to put him to death." [35]

From the home of the rich tax-collector Jesus went his way to Bethany to be the guest of Simon, a healed leper.[36] It was Simon who gave the feast that was to immortalize the name of Mary, the redeemed harlot. She was not a guest—women were not invited—but she was a person determined to demonstrate her gratitude just as another Mary had done at the home of another Simon, a Pharisee, when Jesus' feet were anointed.[37] Scholars may differ as to whether or not it was the same Mary,[38] but whether it was or not, the demonstration of humble gratitude was the same. This Mary entered the room with her hair unbound as a harlot, carrying a box of pure nard, an ointment of great price. With it she anointed the head and feet of her Redeemer.[39] His feet she wiped with her flowing hair—a simple act of great humility. To Judas the gesture was a waste. This ointment was worth 300 denarii (about $60)—a very considerable sum. "Could it not have been sold and the money given to the poor?" asked Judas. The voice of the thief who pilfered the disciples' money box spoke,[40] but to Jesus she had "done a beautiful thing. . . . And truly, I say to you, wherever the gospel is preached in the whole world, what she has done will be told in memory of her." [41] Indeed, in the fifth century St. Chrysostom said:

The memory of what she did, did not fade, but Persians, Indians, Scythians, Thracians, Sauromatians, the race of Moors and the dwellers in the British Isles blaze abroad what was done in Judea by stealth in a house by a woman that had been a harlot.[42]

The feast over, the triumphant procession began, a procession that was to lead not only to the sacred portals of the temple but, before the week was over, to the prisoner's dock of the Great Sanhedrin.

V

JESUS LEFT Simon's house to make his way to the temple, along the old road that leads from Bethany through Bethpage, down over the slopes of the Mount of Olives to the Garden of Gethsemane and across the Kidron Valley to the Golden Gate of the wall of Jerusalem. Today thousands of devout Christians make a pilgrimage over this road on Palm Sunday each year as a memorial to the triumphant entry into Jerusalem, but this procession ends at the Garden of Gethsemane not the temple.

No doubt pilgrims on their way to the Passover had brought news of all that had been happening on the way from Jericho to Bethpage. The news was received in varying ways. There were those to whom Jesus was a Messiah to deliver them out of bondage, to free them from the foreign yoke that bore so heavily on their necks. There were those whose wrath was inflamed—those who saw in him one who could destroy all the cherished vested perquisites of office. To the former he was a Saviour, to the latter, a malefactor.

From Bethpage on the Mount of Olives the view of Jerusalem in those days was a magnificent one—the Jerusalem over which Jesus had wept. The Mount of Olives was still covered with olive trees. Just across the Kidron Valley, the temple rebuilt by Herod the Great was one of the most beautiful structures in the whole world, and one that accommodated 21,000 people. The Antonia and Herod's palace were there and the great viaduct over the deep Tyropean Valley connected the temple courts with Mount Zion. An inspiring sight it must have been. Along the road that led to Bethpage the people had come by hundreds, maybe by thousands. They came to proclaim a king, but Jesus came to Jerusalem not as a conquering king but as a servant riding on the colt of an ass, the dual symbol of peace and humility.

> Lo, your king comes to you;
> triumphant and victorious is he,
> humble and riding on an ass,
> on a colt the foal of an ass.[1]

As Jesus entered Jerusalem thronged with people as it was on all great feast days, old Annas the high priest and his confederates were doing a thriving trade not only in objects of sacrifice—doves, goats and lambs—but exchange as well. Everyone who had attained the age of twenty-one years was required to pay annually a half-shekel into the sacred treasury. The Hebrew half-shekel was the only one that was acceptable as an offering to Jehovah. The thousands of pilgrims from abroad brought with them coins from Egypt, Persia, Greece, Rome and every country where Jews lived and coins were minted. Those from Judea brought different denominations of currency.

The money changers of the temple provided the necessary half-shekel—a service gladly rendered at a profit.

The whole business of engrafting onto the devotional life of his people a lucrative commercial business for the enrichment of their spiritual leaders was odious to the mind of Jesus. It violated everything he taught and lived for and everything he was prepared to die for. Notwithstanding that the objects of his attacks were those very persons who were at that time plotting his destruction, Jesus struck out for a righteous cause. He not only spoke but he acted. Armed with a whip, he went in to the concessions of sacrilege and there drove out the malignant agents of religious corruption. This was a demonstration of no mean significance. It was not so much an attack on the individuals engaged in the trade as it was on the evil practice of degrading spiritual things, a practice that was a relic of paganism with no place in the Jewish religion. In the words of Jeremiah he charged, with justification, that the house of prayer had become a den of robbers.[2] The temple area purged, Jesus returned to his peaceful mission of teaching and healing.

Events of that last fateful week were accelerating to a climax and as they did two things stood out with great clarity: the ruling Jewish authorities were determined to end Jesus' ministry by his immediate death, and at the same time they had grave misgivings about their own security: they feared the multitudes. In these circumstances any action taken must necessarily be swift, be of certain finality, and preferably have a cloak of legality. To this end the chief priests and elders took council.

The last Tuesday, on entering the temple Jesus was at once challenged by the elders, who sought incriminating evidence. "By what authority are you doing these things, and who gave you this authority?" [3] This question was an astute one designed to invite an answer that would be capable of an interpretation to suit the purposes of its authors. Any answer might well serve to found a charge of sorcery or blasphemy, both of which were capital offences under the Jewish law. With the skill of a scholar of the law and one who knew men, Jesus answered, himself asking a question: "I also will ask you a question; and if you tell me the answer, then I also will tell you by what authority I do these things. The baptism of John, whence was it? From heaven or from men?" This put his interrogators in grave difficulty. "If we say, 'From heaven,' he will say to us, 'Why then did you not believe him?' But if we say, 'From men,'" we will have to reckon with a multitude of followers who believe him to be a real prophet. Ignominiously they had recourse to the haven of the defeated witness: "We do not know." Jesus terminated the discussion quite simply. "Neither will I tell you by what authority I do these things." [4]

Jesus returned to the attack, this time speaking in parables. There could be no doubt in the minds of those who heard him against whom the parable of the two sons in the vineyard was directed. No one could doubt whom he meant when he referred to the son who said "I go, sir," but did not go. It was not any one man but a class of men, many of whom were at that very moment seeking means to bring about his death. Nevertheless in clear and strong language he pointed up his indictment: "Truly, I say to you, the tax collectors and the harlots go into the kingdom of God before you. For John came to you in the way of righteousness, and you did not believe him, but the tax collectors and the harlots believed him; and even when you saw it, you did not afterward repent and believe him." Speaking in another parable, Jesus pressed the attack. This time it was the one of the owner of the vineyard whose servants were killed by the tenants and when he sent his son he was likewise killed. He concluded: "Therefore I tell you, the kingdom of God will be taken away from you and given to a nation producing the fruits of it." [5] The chief priests and the Pharisees well knew they were the target against whom these parables were directed: ". . . they perceived that he was speaking about them. But when they tried to arrest him, they feared the multitudes, because they held him to be a prophet." [6] The time was not yet ripe for action. The case required more preparation.

It was a strange combination that now took up the interrogation. The disciples of the Pharisees joined forces with the Herodians, a political party with whom they had little common interests but a desire to be rid of Jesus. They sought to "entangle him" with honeyed words as a cover for a well-laid legal trap: "Teacher, we know that you are true, and teach the way of God truthfully, and care for no man; for you do not regard the position of men." [7] The events of the first three days of that week had surely demonstrated beyond a doubt that Jesus regarded not the position of men. These flattering words were a mere prelude to a shrewd question: "Tell us, then, what you think. Is it lawful to pay taxes to Caesar, or not?" [8] How well the combination of Pharisaic and Herodian minds worked. Such a question is always dear to the heart of every skilful cross-examiner. No matter which way it is answered the answer will suit the purpose of him who propounded it. If Jesus' answer was, "It is lawful" the answer could be used to stir up distrust among those who believed in him. All Jews loathed the Romans and their taxes. If he answered, "It is unlawful," the answer could be used against him on a charge of treason, when the time came for confirmation of any death sentence that might be imposed by the Jewish court. With clear logic and precise legality, Jesus demonstrated the difference between legal obligations and spiritual obligations by simple reference to a Roman coin: "Render . . . to Caesar the things that are Caesar's, and to God the things that are God's." [9]

The Pharisees and Herodians surrendered their task to emissaries who had come from the Sadducees. Ecclesiastically and theologically the Pharisees and Sadducees were in wide disagreement. But on one thing they agreed—Jesus had exposed to view the corrupt practices of their ecclesiastical leaders. They both had a burning desire to guard with vigilance all the vested interests they enjoyed in the fruits of devotion to every letter of the law.

The snare that was set this time was one fabricated from a combination of law and theology. Although Sadducees did not believe in a resurrection of the body, nevertheless they attempted to confound Jesus with the doctrine of the resurrection and the requirements of the Mosaic code concerning levirate marriage. The code provided that if brothers live together and one die without leaving a son, the wife of the dead brother should not marry out of the family to a stranger but her husband's brother should take her "as his wife, and perform the duty of a husband's brother to her." Thus the first son born to her would have the family name and it would not be "blotted out of Israel." [10] The question propounded was: If seven brothers died in succession leaving no children and each in succession took the deceased brother's widow as his wife and she outlived the seventh, to which of the seven brothers would she be wife at the resurrection? [11]

The Sadducees in their turn were frustrated. Jesus' reply was simple but significant. "You are wrong, because you know neither the scriptures nor the power of God." Mosaic law did not say that the brother was to marry the deceased brother's wife. His brother was to take the widow as his wife and perform the duty, not of a husband, but of a husband's brother. The brother was to be the father of a son to perpetuate the name of the deceased brother in his own name. ". . . in the resurrection, they neither marry nor are given in marriage." [12]

The Pharisees hearing that the Sadducees had been silenced returned to the interrogation. This time they enlisted the services of a lawyer from one of their own number. "Teacher, which is the great commandment in the law?" [13] The answer to this question was simply given by quoting from Deuteronomy and Leviticus: "You shall love the lord your God with all your heart, and with all your soul, and with all your mind." [14] "And a second is like it, you shall love your neighbor as yourself."[15] All the agents of the Pharisees, the Sadducees and the Herodians had failed in their missions. They had nothing to report. Every one had been worsted in every encounter and "no one was able to answer him a word, nor from that day did any one dare to ask him any more questions." [16]

Turning to the people, Jesus delivered a still more devastating indictment of those who were plotting to kill him: "The scribes and the Pharisees sit on Moses' seat; so practise and observe whatever they tell you. . ." No sedition preached here— a clear injunction to obey the highest authority in Jewish law. Then follows a charge intended to strip hypocrisy and corruption from all sacred things. Do not do as the Pharisees do, "for they preach, but do not practise. They bind heavy burdens, hard to bear, and lay them on men's shoulders; but they themselves will not move them with their finger. They do all their deeds to be seen by men; for they make their phylacteries broad and their fringes long, . . ." [17] (A phylactery is a small leather container holding parchment inscribed with four passages of scripture worn on the forehead and left arm during

34

morning prayers as a reminder to keep the law.) ". . . they love the place of honor at feasts and the best seats in the synagogues, and salutations in the market places, . . ." [18]

> Woe to you, scribes and Pharisees, hypocrites! for you traverse sea and land to make a single proselyte, you make him twice as much a child of hell as yourselves. Woe to you, blind guides, who say, 'If any one swears by the temple, it is nothing; but if any one swears by the gold of the temple, he is bound by his oath.' You blind men! For which is greater, the gold or the temple that has made the gold sacred? [19]

The form of sacred oaths which played such a large part in the lives of those in authority was denuded of its sham. In devastating language the hypocrisy of the tithing system was exposed:

> Woe to you, scribes and Pharisees, hypocrites! for you tithe mint and dill and cummin, and have neglected the weightier matters of the law, justice and mercy and faith; . . . You blind guides, straining out a gnat and swallowing a camel! Woe to you, scribes and Pharisees, hypocrites! for you cleanse the outside of the cup and of the plate, but inside they are full of extortion and rapacity. . . . Woe to you, scribes and Pharisees, hypocrites! for you are like whitewashed tombs, which outwardly appear beautiful, but within they are full of dead men's bones and all uncleanness. So you also outwardly appear righteous to men, but within you are full of hypocrisy and iniquity. Woe to you, scribes and Pharisees, hypocrites! for you build the tombs of the prophets and adorn the monuments of the righteous, saying, 'If we had lived in the days of our fathers, we would not have taken part with them in shedding the blood of the prophets.' Thus you witness against yourselves, that you are sons of those who murdered the

35

prophets. Fill up, then, the measure of your fathers. You serpents, you brood of vipers, how are you to escape being sentenced to hell? [20]

Having finished Jesus left the temple and went his way over the Mount of Olives to Bethpage there to spend Tuesday night.

It is little wonder that a meeting was convened at the palace of the high priest on Wednesday morning. This time events took a more violent turn. The agents sent out by those who would ultimately constitute the court that was to try Jesus had failed to get the desired evidence to support a capital charge of any kind. The plan to clothe their evil designs with judicial respectability was defeated by the requirements not only of their own law but those of the Roman law.

Those gathered at the palace of Caiaphas "took counsel together in order to arrest Jesus by stealth and kill him." [21] There is no suggestion here that there should be a trial. A trial there must not be unless there was evidence sufficient to support a capital charge and that evidence was wanting. Any semblance of judicial procedure was completely abandoned. The plan adopted was to seize Jesus and to kill him in secret. It may well have been the merciful provisions of the Hebrew law, which we shall later discuss, that drove the chief priests and elders to discard their judicial robes and don the masks of conspirators as they gathered together with Caiaphas that Wednesday morning. They determined to kill him, but "not during the feast, lest there be a tumult among the people." [22]

The events now took their determined course. Death must come and it must come quickly. With the Passover only two days away all that was to be accomplished must be achieved before the Passover began at sunset on Friday. In the plot to

36

take Jesus by stealth and kill him a ready accomplice was found in none other than one of the twelve disciples. Judas, the only disciple that was not of Galilean origin,[23] offered his services, but at a price. For thirty pieces of silver his name was made a timeless symbol of treachery.

Thursday was a day of intimate spiritual intercourse with those who followed Jesus. It was the day when he would eat the Paschal supper. There seems to have been some secrecy about where the sacred feast would be observed. It may be that the secrecy was intended to confound Judas who was at that very time in the pay of the high priest and seeking to betray Jesus "in the absence of the multitude." [24] The sign to direct the guests to the chosen place was a man carrying a jar of water on his head—something quite unusual in the Middle East. Such tasks were usually performed by women. The man with the jar took them to a well-furnished guest room. There the feast was eaten. Even such a sacred feast could not escape life's trivialities. The disciples got into a controversy over the seating arrangements. A dispute arose over who was the greatest. Jesus disposed of this controversy very simply—the one who serves is the greatest. The dispute settled, the meal proceeded and was concluded with all the attendant ritual. When a hymn was sung Jesus left the upper room and with his little band wended his way across the Kidron to the Garden of Gethsemane, a place of great beauty—there to pray.

No more convenient time could be found for the conspirators to strike. Night had fallen. The crowds that during that eventful week had hailed Jesus' entry into Jerusalem with cries of "Hosanna" and who had strewn his path with palms had all departed to their lodgings. The throngs that had heard his teaching in the temple and witnessed his withering attacks on religious hypocrisy were all dispersed to their homes. This was

37

the time when Jesus could be disposed of with a minimum of tumult.

So the chief priests and the elders mobilized their own great multitude—a mob of ruffians armed with clubs and swords—among them some small detachment of Roman soldiers. Annas' brigands were diverted from robbing lesser priests of their dues at the threshing-floor to another task. They were to take him. This was no ordinary arrest. It was part of a well-laid plan to commit murder. Those who came were not officers of the law in the true sense. They were members of a band who required a sign to identify their man. One cannot conceive that any regular officer of the law would have had to resort to bribery to identify Jesus. He had been a central figure in the courts of the temple for nearly a week. Judas bargained for the sign, "The one I shall kiss is the man; . . ." [25] At the proper time he fulfilled his assignment as the paid informer—". . . he came up to Jesus at once and said, 'Hail Master!' And he kissed him. Jesus said to him, 'Friend, why are you here?' " [26] The whole episode is well stamped as the execution of a plan that had been laid to take Jesus and kill him secretly.

Something interrupted the course of events. It may be that it was the impulsive Peter who deflected the course of history. The seizure of Jesus aroused his anger. Recognizing Malchus, a slave of the high priest, as one of the ruffians, Peter drew his sword and cut off the slave's ear. The dismembered ear would directly identify the slave's master with the plot. It may be that it was Jesus' appeal to his assailants that struck a note of caution in the hearts of those who were employed in the unlawful enterprise. "Have you come out as against a robber, with swords and clubs to capture me? Day after day I sat in the temple teaching, and you did not seize me." [27]

It may be that it was realized that the events of the early days of the week had demonstrated that there was in Jerusalem

38

very great numbers of Jesus' followers and among them many revolutionary Galileans. Rome would have to be reckoned with if there was an uprising among the people. It may be that it was the presence of the Roman soldiers that prevented a summary execution. On these matters one can only speculate. Whatever may have happened, events did not take their charted course. Jesus was not killed in secret nor was he taken to a court of justice.

The assassins' plot having miscarried, its authors found themselves in a situation that was driving them to desperation. In less than twenty-four hours the Sabbath would begin and with it the feast of the Passover. The rulers, who were prepared to commit murder, would not commit murder during the feast day, not so much because of their scruples but because of the scruples of the people. Having arrested Jesus, they now had to act quickly; so they took him by night to Annas. Annas was a former high priest and the father-in-law of Caiaphas, the ruling high priest.

VI

WHEN JESUS entered the city, the cries of "Hosanna to the son of David!" coming from the crowds that lined the way had filled all the high priests with apprehension. The ruling high priest, standing as he did at the vertex of ecclesiastical authority, held a lofty but tenuous position. He owed his appointment to Herod Antipas and to Pilate, and at their will he could be deposed. To have attained that office he needed all his wealth to meet the demands of an avaricious governor and a Herodian prince, both of whom were quite willing to sell it to

39

the highest bidder.[1] But the candidates for the office could well afford to bid high. Great riches were accumulated from the tithes that were the dues of the priests.[2]

Caiaphas, who presided over the trial of Jesus in the Jewish court, was head of the council of chief priests. His chief qualification for his office would appear to be that he was the son-in-law of Annas. He had been appointed to the office by Gratius just before the latter was succeeded by Pontius Pilate.[3] Vitellius, Pilate's successor, deprived him of his office not because he condemned Jesus but to make way for his brother-in-law, a son of Annas. It was no accident that all of Annas' five sons and his son-in-law wore the robes of the high priest at one time or another, since old Annas wielded the political and ecclesiastical power. Neither was it an accident that not only his son-in-law Caiaphas but his son Annas were both destined to make a mockery of judicial procedure.[4]

No better language can be used to describe the evil character of Annas than that of Josephus:

> But as for the high priest Ananias[5] he increased in glory every day and this to a great degree, and had obtained the favour and esteem of the citizens in a signal manner; for he was a great hoarder up of money; he therefore cultivated the friendship of Albinus, and of the high priest, by making them presents; he also had servants who were very wicked, who joined themselves to the boldest sort of the people, and went to the thrashing-floors, and took away the tithes that belonged to the priests by violence, and did not refrain from beating such as would not give these tithes to them. So the other high priests acted in the like manner, as did those his servants, without anyone being able to prohibit them; so that [some of the] priests, that of old were wont to be supported with those tithes, died for want of food.[6]

40

A taunt song in the Talmud has served as an epitaph for Annas and a reminder of his instruments of terror:

A plague on the house of Boethus: a plague on their clubs!
A plague on the house of Annas; a plague on their spying![7]

In addition to the tithes and first fruits, there were many other lucrative perquisites of the priestly office. With them went a monopoly in doves, goats and lambs necessary for the sacrifices on the great feast days. Every sacrifice offered had to be without blemish, and for those pilgrims whose offerings were condemned and for those who came from afar, acceptable offerings had to be found. All these the priests were ready to supply, but at a price.

The perquisites did not end there. To the priests went a share of the offerings that were not consumed on the altar. In many cases only a small portion of the carcass ever reached the altar. In the sin offerings the fat only was consumed, while the priests acquired the carcass. Of thank offerings they collected the breast and right shoulder and of burnt offerings the skin, affording to them a lucrative trade in hides.[8]

Annas, steeped as he was in the law and politics of the Jewish people, may well have been the architect of the schemes to get evidence to support a conviction for a capital offence. He no doubt knew that they had failed. True, the disciples had been seen plucking the ears of corn on the Sabbath, but Jesus worsted his accusers on that charge. All efforts to get evidence of sorcery, blasphemy, treason and being a false prophet had failed. In every encounter those who would entrap him were defeated. Nowhere was there evidence that he taught disobedience to the laws of God or man.

Annas was the one who was now in a dilemma. Peter's

assault on the slave had publicly connected the high priest with the seizure of Jesus. Annas knew too well all the administrative technicality of the Hebraic criminal law. He must have known that secret assassination was now out of the question. It was better that the destruction of Jesus be given a cloak of respectability. Some form of judicial procedure was to be the cloak, no matter how stained and saturated with illegality. The Sanhedrin was called in an emergency session to sit during the night. For the Sanhedrin evidence there must be, and Annas took to himself the task of securing evidence where others had failed. He questioned Jesus about his disciples and his teaching. All Annas' questions were answered with quiet dignity:

> A. I have spoken openly to the world; I have always taught in synagogues and in the temple, where all Jews come together; I have said nothing secretly. Why do you ask me? Ask those who have heard me, what I said to them; they know what I said.

Then followed a beating of the prisoner to extract a confession. One of the high priest's officers struck Jesus with his hand and admonished him. "Is that how you answer the high priest?" Even though Caiaphas was the high priest that year, it was the common custom to refer to a former high priest as a high priest. The beating brought forth a simple, logical request for proper evidence:

> A. If I have spoken wrongly, bear witness to the wrong; but if I have spoken rightly, why do you strike me?

Nothing was to be accomplished by private interrogation. The whole proceeding before Annas was illegal from beginning to end according to the Hebraic law. Every accused had a right to be free from any private or personal interrogation until he was sent for public trial.[9] Friday's dawn was approaching. There could be no further delay. Annas had Jesus bound and sent him to Caiaphas to stand his trial before the Great Sanhedrin.[10]

VII

THE SANHEDRIN as it then was may have been a reflection of the council of seventy elders and officers called together to assist Moses.[1] If it was, it was but a dim reflection adapted to another conception of government and administration, one that was the product of Grecian influence.[2] Its members were men of wealth and power. In theory it was theocratic. In no sense was it democratic.[3] As far as the internal government of the Jewish people was concerned, the Great Synhedrion (a Greek term meaning assembly) exercised the final authority in all matters—religious, social, political, legislative and judicial. Ultimately the body was known as the Sanhedrin. The native Hebrew term was *Bet din Hagadal,* or High Council of the High Court.[4]

The supreme body consisted of seventy-one members with the high priest at its head. Its chief function was that of a court. It sat in Jerusalem and under it were lesser Sanhedrins, each consisting of twenty-three members. Two of these lesser bodies sat in Jerusalem, while others sat in the larger cities. Beneath them all were village courts consisting of three members.[5]

About 55 B.C. Gabinius divided the whole Jewish territory so that it was governed by five Sanhedrins, "three of which were allotted to Judea, those of Jerusalem, Gazara and Jericho." [6] This distribution of power was changed by Caesar ten years later with the appointment of Herod the Great, who himself had been tried before the Sanhedrin on a charge of murder. After his appointment as King of Judea, Herod's first demonstration of authority was to put all the members of the Sanhedrin to death.[7]

Following this massacre the Sanhedrin was composed of those who were more tractable to the Herodian will but after the death of Herod and of Archelaus, his successor, the Sanhedrin in Jerusalem became an aristocracy composed of former high priests and religious leaders (the elders) under the direction of the high priest. In it Sadducean influence predominated. Although the Sanhedrin functioned as the supreme judicial authority over Jewish affairs, its powers were limited in capital cases during the Roman occupation. No sentence of death could be carried out until it was confirmed by the Roman governor.[8]

When assembled, the members of the court sat in a half-circle (half a threshing-floor) so they could see one another. Two scribes or judges stood, one on the right and one on the left. One of these scribes wrote down what was said in favour of acquittal and the other noted what was said in favour of conviction. In some cases there was a third who wrote down what was said both for acquittal and conviction. Before the court sat three rows of disciples (students) or sages. From the first row were drawn substitute judges if any were needed to fill vacancies. In each case the place of the disciple chosen to sit as a judge was filled by one from the second row whose place was filled by one from the third row. A member of the congregation was chosen to take the place of the disciple taken from the third row, but he did not sit in his place "but he sat in the place that was proper for him." [9]

In all criminal cases the Hebrew law was strict and it was particularly so in capital cases. The death penalty was pre-

44

scribed for a whole catalogue of offences ranging all the way from "being a stubborn and rebellious son" to murder. These offences included blasphemy,[10] profaning the Sabbath after warning,[11] sorcery,[12] idolatry,[13] and being a false prophet.[14] Four types of execution were prescribed according to the character of the offence: stoning, burning, strangling and beheading. These were said to be in descending order of the gravity of the offence.[15] If an accused was found to be liable to two death penalties, the law prescribed that he be punished by the more severe.[16] Crucifixion was not a penalty authorized by Hebrew law. It was a Roman form of punishment.

Severe as was the text of the Hebrew law, its rigours were greatly mitigated by humane rules of administration, and nowhere were they more humane than in capital cases. Judges were adjured to test the evidence. "The more a judge tests the evidence the more is he deserving of praise. . . ."[17] Detailed directions were given to judges to guide them in accepting or rejecting evidence.

In every capital case the witness was admonished:

> Perchance ye will say what is but supposition or hearsay or at secondhand, or [ye may say in yourselves], We heard it from a man that was trustworthy. Or perchance ye do not know that we shall prove you by examination and inquiry? Know ye, moreover, that capital cases are not as non-capital cases: in non-capital cases a man may pay money and so make atonement, but in capital cases the witness is answerable for the blood of him [that is wrongfully condemned] and the blood of his posterity [that should have been born to him] to the end of the world. . . . If any man has caused a single soul to perish from Israel scripture imputes it to him as though he had caused a whole world to perish; and if any man saves alive a single soul from Israel scripture imputes it to him as though he had saved alive a whole world.[18]

45

No one might be found guilty except on the evidence of two witnesses.[19] A false witness was himself liable to the same punishment prescribed for the offence with which the accused was charged.[20] If one witness contradicted another during the inquiry either on examination or cross-examination, the evidence of both became invalid.[21] If a witness had anything of substance to say in favour of acquittal, he was required to be heard and detained throughout the whole trial. The accused had a right to give evidence in his own defence (a right that was not generally accorded to an accused in England until 1898). A majority of two in the court was required for a conviction while a majority of one was sufficient for an acquittal. A member of a court who once voted for acquittal was not permitted to change his vote, but a member who voted for conviction was permitted to vote for acquittal at any time before the sentence was carried out.

Even the disciples (students) or sages who attended the court were permitted to argue in favour of acquittal but not for conviction. In such cases the disciple was brought up to sit among the members of the court and remained with them throughout the day.[22] When there was a conviction, sentence could not be passed on the same day. The members of the court were required to go in pairs, eating very little and drinking no wine, to discuss the matter all night and come together the following morning. On the following morning commencing with the most junior member of the court lest he be influenced by his seniors, each was required to make his declaration. Those in favour of acquittal would say: "I declared him innocent yesterday and I still declare him innocent." And those in favour of conviction would say: "I declared him guilty yesterday and I still declare him guilty." He who favoured conviction might afterwards acquit, but he who favoured acquittal might not retract and favour conviction.[23] It was said, "A Sanhedrin that puts one man to death in a week of years is called 'destructive.' " [24]

The safeguards against the execution of an innocent man did not end with the judgment of the court and with the sentence. The law required the execution, which was carried out on the same day as the sentence was passed, to take place outside the walls.[25] When the condemned man was taken from the place of judgment, a sentry with a towel in his hand was posted at the door of the judgment hall. Another was mounted on a horse at a post where he could be in reach of the place of execution but close enough to the judgment hall to see the sentry with the towel. A herald led the procession, calling out the name of the condemned man and announcing the offence for which he was convicted and the sentence imposed, adding: "If any man knoweth aught in favour of his acquittal let him come and plead it." [26] If it came to the attention of the court that anyone, whether a member of the court or not, wished to advance some further argument, the sentry with the towel signalled the horseman and the latter thereupon halted the procession and returned the prisoner to the court. Even if the prisoner during the procession said: "I have somewhat to argue in favour of my acquittal," the law required that he be brought back for further trial, be it four or five times, if there was substance in what he had to say.[27]

The role of the witness for the prosecution was not ended when he gave his evidence. Where the prisoner was sentenced to be stoned, the first witness was the one required to drop the first stone from twice the height of the man. If the first stone did not cause death, the second witness was required to drop the next stone. If the condemned man still lived, he was stoned at the hands of all the people.[28]

The fact that the Sanhedrin could not sit on the Sabbath

47

or feast days largely controlled the course of events during the last hours of Jesus' life. In order to complete the trial and have the execution over before Friday at sundown, the court assembled in the night. The prisoner was there, but there was neither formal accusation nor witnesses. What was to have had the appearance of a trial soon became an inquisition. The members of the court on whom rested one of the most sacred of all duties known to the Hebrew law—to sit in judgment—discarded the injunction of their law to "test the evidence," and connived to pervert justice. They "sought false testimony against Jesus that they might put him to death, . . ." [29]

False witnesses there were, but their evidence was of no account: "And some stood up and bore false witness against him, saying, 'We heard him say, "I will destroy this temple that is made with hands, and in three days I will build another, not made with hands."'" [30] These witnesses, like most false witnesses, did not agree. [31] Since they failed to agree, their evidence according to Jewish law was as if it had not been given. Jesus' accusers were surely hard put for an accusation that might support a capital offence when they entertained such evidence. This evidence may have been advanced in a feeble effort to support a charge of sorcery, or as is more likely it was intended to support a charge of blasphemy. The statement that Jesus would destroy the temple and in three days raise one not made with hands was capable of two interpretations. Jesus was attacking Jewish institutions or, on the other hand, he was making a claim to supernatural power. In either case such a claim was capable of being interpreted as blasphemy. In the accusation against Stephen a few months later the law was so interpreted. His offence was that he had been heard to say that "Jesus of Nazareth shall destroy this place and shall change the customs which Moses delivered to us." [32]

Blasphemy according to Jewish law is not mere profanity.

48

It is an insult directed against God—a sort of treason against the Deity. This is one of the crimes that has given ecclesiastical judges throughout history wide latitude and great scope to give vent to their passions. The offence of blasphemy was a very necessary part of the Hebraic law because the Hebrew common-wealth was in theory a theocracy. All its priests, prophets, judges and kings were held to have been mere courtiers and ministers of the invisible King whose word was Israel's constitution and law. The verbal renunciation of God was in the strict sense high treason, and any attempt to subvert the institutions of his government was constructive treason and thus blasphemy.[33] Whatever interpretation might have been put on the evidence of the witnesses with reference to the declarations about the destruction of the temple, even to Caiaphas and his court, it did not support a charge of blasphemy. The cocks were beginning to crow. No matter how malignant the whole proceedings were, the letter of the law must be complied with. The verdict must be reached before dawn so that the Sanhedrin might re-convene in the morning according to the law.

At this stage Caiaphas forsook his role as a judge, and vio-lating all the rules of Hebraic procedure, he undertook to ac-complish what his minions had failed to do—to get Jesus to make a self-convicting statement. In some countries, before the accused is sent for public trial he is taken before a magistrate to be questioned in private. No such procedure was known to Hebrew law. Until the case was established by the evidence of two or three witnesses given publicly, one standing trial for crime was not only presumed to be innocent but to be unac-cused.[34] It was the evidence of the leading witnesses that con-stituted the charge. When they spoke and agreed, their evidence constituted the indictment.[35] There being no evidence and hence no charge, Caiaphas stood up and heaped illegality upon

49

illegality by calling upon Jesus to testify against himself. Caiaphas administered the most solemn oath known to the Jews: "I adjure you by the living God, tell us if you are the Christ, the Son of God." Jesus replied: "You have said so. But I tell you, hereafter you will see the Son of man seated at the right hand of Power, and coming on the clouds of heaven."[36] There are two other versions of this interrogation in the gospels. Mark quotes Jesus as replying: "I am; and you will see the Son of man sitting at the right hand of Power, and coming with the clouds of heaven."[37] Luke gives a version which is still slightly different in context and time. He puts the interrogation at the time when the Sanhedrin re-convened in the morning, which is not likely. This is the record taken from Luke:

Q. If you are the Christ, tell us.
A. If I tell you, you will not believe; and if I ask you, you will not answer. But from now on the Son of man shall be seated at the right hand of the power of God.
Q. Are you Son of God, then?
A. You say that I am.[38]

Whichever version is the correct one, with great dexterity Caiaphas had framed his question so that no matter how the question was answered his determined purpose would be fulfilled. If Jesus refused to answer, his divine mission would have been destroyed; likewise, if his answer was a denial it would have been a confession that he was a false prophet; if he admitted his Messiahship the admission, no matter how obtained, would have been interpreted as blasphemy and used to support a declaration that he was worthy of death. No doubt Caiaphas felt the Roman governor would not concern himself with investigating how the evidence was adduced in the Hebrew court.

The course of the trial had now crystallized. The intention

was that the conviction should be for blasphemy, but the proper procedure in such cases created difficulties and it was not to be followed in this case. The Mishnah sets out the procedure thus:

'The blasphemer' is not culpable unless he pronounces the Name itself. R. Joshua b. Karha says: On every day (of the trial) they examined the witnesses with a substituted name, (such as) 'May Jose smite Jose'. When sentence was to be given they did not declare him guilty of death (on the grounds of evidence given) with the substituted name, but they sent out all the people and asked the chief among the witnesses and said to him, 'Say expressly what thou heardest', and he says it; and the judges stand up on their feet and rend their garments, and they may not mend them again. And the second witness says 'I also heard the like', and the third says, 'I also heard the like'.[39]

All these strictures of the law were to be forgotten and the traditional legal procedure disregarded. No vote of the members of the court was taken before Caiaphas announced the verdict—he "tore his robes, and said, 'He has uttered blasphemy. Why do we still need witnesses? You have now heard his blasphemy. What is your judgment?' "[40] Caiaphas had himself given the judgment and performed the sacred rite. It would have been a courageous junior member of the Sanhedrin who, in the presence of Caiaphas and old Annas and all his sons, would have stood out for acquittal after that judgment was given. None did. The vote was taken. All members of the council answered: "He deserves death."[41] But the sentence of death they could not pass. Judgment was given and justice was doubly degraded. The Jewish law provided that no prolonged death might be inflicted on anyone, nor could a person condemned to death be previously scourged.[42] But Jesus was spat upon and beaten. Notwithstanding that the court was prepared to blot out the whole spirit of the law, the letter was to be adhered to in matters that meant little. The court adjourned to re-convene in the morning.

During the night no small drama of pathos and human frailty was enacted. From the time of his arrest, Peter and John had followed Jesus at a distance. They did not leave him at the house of Annas. At the Sanhedrin Peter was there but in the courtyard, not in the courtroom. It was cold at that hour in the morning and Peter joined the doorkeepers, porters and other servants who were grouped around a brazier warming them- selves. A mischievous maid who had no doubt been about Jerusalem that week recognized Peter as one who was "with the Nazarene Jesus" and so accosted him. Peter may have been moved by fear of recognition as the one who had cut off the ear of the slave of the high priest, or it may be that he was merely terrified as he found himself utterly alone in a hostile crowd. He denied any connection with Jesus or his teaching, not once but three times. The episode was interrupted as Jesus was led from the judgment hall to the guardroom. Jesus looked on Peter. That look was enough. Peter wept. The servants went about their affairs. They were no longer concerned with Peter. There were more exciting things to take their attention.

When morning came the court re-assembled and after consultation they bound Jesus and led him away and delivered him to Pilate, the governor.[43]

The Hebrew trial had closed. Steeped as it was in illegality, it had been a mockery of judicial procedure throughout. Jesus was unlawfully arrested and unlawfully interrogated in secret by one of the highest ranking members of the court, one who was to sit among his judges. The court was unlawfully con- vened by night. No lawful charge supported by the evidence of two witnesses was ever formulated. When he was questioned by Caiaphas Jesus was, according to Hebrew law, innocent. No charge had been laid against him. As he stood at the bar of justice he was unlawfully sworn as witness against himself. He was unlawfully condemned to death on words from his own mouth. "Our law," says Marmonidis, "condemns no one to death upon his own confession." "It is a fundamental principle with us," says Bartenora, "that no one can damage himself by what he says in judgment." [44] There was no echo of the voice of Amos in the judgment hall that night: ". . . let justice roll down like waters, and righteousness like an everflowing stream." [45] Nor did the judges of Jesus remember Micah's injunction to all judges: ". . . what doth the Lord require of thee, but to do justly, and to love mercy, and to walk humbly with thy God?" [46]

VIII

JUST ABOUT the time that Jesus commenced his ministry, Pontius Pilate was appointed Procurator of Judea. In the name of the emperor, Pilate exercised executive, military and judicial power. From his decisions there was no appeal except to Caesar. He has been described in a letter, which Philo said was written by Agrippa the First, as an "unbending and relentless hard character," and has been charged with "corruptibility, violence, robberies, ill treatment of the people, grievances, continual executions without even the form of a trial, needless and intolerable cruelties." [1]

With traditional Roman wisdom, former procurators had respected the Jewish law which forbade making or displaying any image.[2] Pilate may not have intended to taunt the Jewish people by his first official act, but taunt them he did when he set up by night effigies of Caesar in Jerusalem. He was forthwith taught a lesson he remembered three years later. A great deputation of Jews went at once from Jerusalem to Caesarea to implore Pilate to remove the effigies. For five days the deputation persevered in its importunities, lying immovable in the market-place throughout the day. On the sixth day with an army of soldiers concealed near by, Pilate took his place on a judgment seat that had been prepared for him in the marketplace. Upon the Jews coming to repeat their petition, the soldiers surrounded the petitioners with drawn swords, threatening them with death unless "they would leave off disturbing him, and go their ways home." The only response the petitioners made to these threats was to throw themselves on the ground and lay bare their necks, saying that "they would take their death very willingly, rather than the wisdom of their laws should be transgressed; . . ." Pilate was not prepared to answer to Caesar at this time for a massacre of this magnitude and not for the last time he capitulated and ordered the offending images to be removed from Jerusalem and brought back to Caesarea.[3]

A still worse political and religious storm broke when Pilate robbed the treasury of the temple and applied the *corban* (money dedicated to God) to build an aqueduct to convey water four hundred furlongs from the Pool of Solomon southwest of Bethlehem to Jerusalem. This time tens of thousands of Jews gathered in Jerusalem to protest against the sacrilege, insisting that he "leave off that design." Having been forewarned of their purpose, Pilate resorted to a piece of cowardly trickery. He disguised armed soldiers in civilian dress and caused them to mingle in the crowd. On a given signal the soldiers beat peaceful and tumultuous citizens alike. ". . . there were a great number of them slain by this means, and others of them ran away wounded. And thus an end was put to this sedition.[4]

It is fair to infer that among those beaten and killed were Galileans who, if there were disturbances at great feasts, were sure to be there, and it is an equally fair inference that it was these Galileans that Luke referred to as "the Galileans whose blood Pilate had mingled with their sacrifices."[5]

Insult upon insult was heaped upon the Jews. Under the pretence of honouring Caesar, richly gilded votive shields engraved with the emperor's name were hung in the palace of Herod in Jerusalem. This may have been a lesser outrage than the introduction of the images, but nonetheless it stirred the passions of the people to exasperation. A horde of Jewish leaders, no doubt including members of the Sanhedrin, joined with four sons of Herod the Great to petition the governor to remove the shields. Pilate obstinately refused. An appeal this time was taken directly to Tiberius himself. Tiberius was not moved by any sympathy for the Jewish people, but he was having no more insurrection than could be avoided. He rebuked Pilate and ordered the offending shields removed.[6] These were the memories that were to course through the uncertain mind of Pilate as he vacillated in his task as a Roman judge when Jesus stood before him for trial.

Pilate had come up, as was his custom, from his official residence at Caesarea to be present in Jerusalem during the feast of the Passover. He did not come out of any respect for the sacred feast, but as a precautionary measure lest there be any disturbance that might have more than local consequences.

To Pilate's palace went the members of the Sanhedrin in the early hours of Friday morning. Within the palace was

Pilate but there, too, were the altars of the Roman gods. Into such a place the Hebrew priests and the doctors (scribes) would not enter during the sacred week, "so that they might not be defiled, . . ." [7] Acceding to the religious scruples of the distinguished body that waited on him, Pilate moved the judgment seat to a convenient place outside the palace, probably to the courtyard. If there was to be a Roman trial, it must be a public one. As he ascended the dais in the improvised judgment hall, he was *Procurator Caesarius,* the symbol and the manifestation of the power of Rome. He was custodian of the only Roman institution that the impact of time was not to erode away to be lost in the mist of history—the Roman law. A poor custodian he proved to be.

The trial opened. The prisoner was brought before the judge. The first question that was asked is the first question that is asked today in every court of Anglo-Saxon heritage and in fact in every court of Roman heritage: "What accusation do you bring against this man?" [8] This at once posed a difficult problem for those judges who had now become Jesus' accusers and prosecutors. The request for the charge made it quite clear that there was to be no formal confirmation of the judgment of the Sanhedrin. It was evident that Pilate intended to do his duty as a dispenser of Roman justice and dispose of the case on its merits. Before the Sanhedrin there had been no accusation. The verdict had determined the charge. The problem that perplexed Jesus' accusers was this: if they said, "We have tried him and found him guilty of blasphemy," Pilate would regard the whole matter as a religious dispute which could well be left to the Jewish court. In that case the Roman governor would not likely ratify any death sentence. So the accusers resorted to equivocation:"If this man were not an evildoer, we would not have handed him over." [9] They were calling for a *pro forma* confirmation of the judgment of the Sanhedrin. Had the Sanhedrin not declared him to be worthy of death? A sense of Roman justice would not permit Pilate to grant such a confirmation, and he evaded the issue with considerable dexterity: "Take him yourselves and judge him by your own law." [10] To the members of the Sanhedrin Pilate's conduct of the proceedings was becoming alarming. He was about to do the very thing they did not want him to do—leave the matter to the Jewish courts. So they changed their strategy. Ceasing to rely on the judgment of the Sanhedrin which found Jesus guilty of blasphemy, they resorted to something which was calculated to stimulate in Pilate a greater interest in the case.

With no reference to the offence for which Jesus had been convicted in the Hebrew court, new accusations were put forward: "We found this man perverting our nation, and forbidding us to give tribute to Caesar, and saying that he himself is Christ a king." [11] The first and second charges were patently false and the third a half-truth presented in such a way as to be entirely false. Taken together, these charges were accusations that Jesus had challenged the authority of the Roman state and attacked its majestic sovereignty. This was *majestatis* (treason), the greatest crime known to the state, and the citizen condemned for that crime was interdicted through fire and water or hanged at an *arbor infelix*.[12]

The Roman procedure required that every accusation of treason against a Roman citizen be made by a written charge and the accused, if a Roman citizen, was entitled to all the protection of a properly conducted Roman trial. A Jew, who was not a Roman citizen, had no such protection. With Jesus before him, Pilate as Procurator of Caesar, had absolute power limited only by his sense of justice.

The proceedings, which had commenced with a formal

57

demand for confirmation of a death sentence, developed into a trial for treason. The Jews were driven on a course they did not want to take because they well knew there was not the necessary evidence to support the charge. They had tried to get evidence to support the first two allegations but failed. Had not Jesus said: "Render unto Caesar the things which are Caesar's"? Pilate must have detected malice in the hearts of the Sanhedrists. When had they ever shown any vigilance in the matter of urging their people to pay Roman taxes? It is not improbable that the Roman Procurator, whose thumb was on the pulse of the development of every Jewish movement, had heard that this very man had been charged by his present accusers of being " a friend of tax-gatherers." Within the last week he had accepted the hospitality of one of the chief tax-gatherers down at Jericho. It is not likely that the movement that had been commenced by John the Baptist and carried on by Jesus, with all the open attack on ecclesiastical corruption, could have passed unnoticed by a man worthy of the confidence of Caesar. Pilate must have discerned that it was from no loyalty to Caesar that the chief priests and elders came with their prisoner at that early hour of the morning, charging that he had been forbidding them to give tribute to Caesar; Pilate well knew that it was out of envy that they had delivered him up.

The third accusation—that Jesus had said he was Christ the King—could not pass unnoticed, even though Pilate did know that it was "out of envy" that he had been brought there. A charge that anyone who had created such an impact on the Jewish people had claimed any rights of temporal power must necessarily be investigated. Since the accused was not a Roman citizen, Pilate as master of his own procedure decided that he would talk to Jesus directly. It may be that he had more than a passing curiosity to talk privately with this man who had that very week spoken with such matchless courage against corruption in Jewish religious affairs. It may be that the events of the week had been much discussed in Pilate's household. There is a tradition that Claudia Procula, Pilate's wife, was a proselyte to the Jewish religion.[13] If this be true, it is also likely that she had heard Jesus teach in the temple during Passion week and had related much of what she had heard to her husband. Entering the praetorium Pilate called Jesus and questioned him:

Q. Are you the King of the Jews?
A. Do you say this of your own accord, or did others say it to you about me? [14]

Jesus was asking, "Do you use the word 'king' in the Roman sense or in the prophetic sense of the Jewish tradition?" Pilate's reply is said by some to indicate irritability, a conclusion the text hardly warrants:

Q. Am I a Jew? Your own nation and the chief priests have handed you over to me; what have you done? [15]

Pilate was merely saying, "I do not know the Jewish traditions. You have been sent here by the members of the Sanhedrin. I don't understand the charge. What claims have you made to kingship?" Jesus' answer was directed to set Pilate's mind at rest as to any claim to a political mission:

A. My kingship is not of this world; if my kingship were of this world, my servants would fight, that I might not be handed over to the Jews [the Sanhedrin]; . . .[16]

Had he not when arrested reprimanded Peter for the use of the sword? Pilate continued to question him:

Q. So you are a king?
A. You say that I am. . . .[17]

59

Jesus followed with a sublime declaration of his eternal purpose:

> For this I was born, and for this I have come into the world, to bear witness to the truth. Every one who is of the truth hears my voice.[18]

Pilate replied, "What is truth?"[19] There is no reason to believe that this was an idle question. It is one that has confounded philosophers from the beginning of time. We do not have the answer if answer was made, but one thing is clear: the interrogation of the prisoner disclosed no crime known to the Roman law. Pilate returned to the courtyard to resume the judgment seat in public. There he gave judgment in as clear and unequivocal terms as judgment could be given. "I find no crime in this man."[20]

That should have been the end of the case and the prisoner should have been discharged and allowed to go his way as a free man, but he was not. The Jewish leaders knew Pilate. Three times before they had bent his will to theirs and they set out to do it again. They well remembered that multitudes of Jews in the market-place of Caesarea had bared their necks to the swords of the Roman soldiers, and defied Pilate's orders until the effigies of Caesar were removed from Jerusalem. Pilate had not forgotten that tens of thousands of devout Jews refused to yield to his demands that they disperse, as they protested his theft of the sacred money of the temple. Nor had he forgotten that as these same Jews were wantonly slaughtered by Roman soldiers, they "boldly" cast "reproaches upon him."[21] Both Pilate and the Sanhedrists would vividly recall that Tiberius himself had reprimanded Pilate for being at the root of the disturbance over the votive shields, which were removed from Herod's palace on the direct orders of Caesar. With all these memories coursing through their heated and excited brains, the Sanhedrist judges and their attendant followers made a tumult in the judgment hall, crying out: "He stirs up the people, teaching throughout all Judea, from Galilee even to this place." [22]

Pilate began to show signs of weakness. He sought to evade his duty. On hearing that Jesus came from Galilee, he thought he saw an avenue of escape. Herod Antipas, the Tetrarch of Galilee, was in Jerusalem at that time. "And when he learned that he belonged to Herod's jurisdiction, he sent him over to Herod, . . ." [23] It was not because Pilate had any fondness for Herod that he abdicated his legal responsibility and his judicial duty. He merely grasped the opportunity to let Herod be accountable to Rome if violence broke out. It may not be unreasonable to assume that Pilate was well acquainted with Herod's distinguished career in disposing of those whom he might find troublesome, just as his father had often done before him.

IX

HEROD ANTIPAS was much more fortunate than his brother Archelaus. True, he had lost his case before Caesar but he had kept his tetrarchy of Galilee and Perea. Antipas inherited much more than a tetrarchy from his father. He inherited a matchless legacy of training in the art of ruthless intrigue and some measure of statesmanship. It is hard to detect when this Herod was just being crafty and when he was practising some sincerity of purpose in statecraft. Unlike Pilate, he showed a

61

very considerable measure of respect for the traditions of Judaism. At each Passover Antipas came from Galilee to Jerusalem with much pomp to attend the ceremonial festivities. It was this respect for Jewish traditions, together with his disrespect for the Jewish marriage laws, that gained him a place, but not a distinguished one, in the history of Christianity.

Antipas' troubles with the marriage laws arose out of a visit to his half-brother Philip in Rome. There Antipas met his brother's wife Herodias who had one thing in common with her husband. Her family had been victims of Herodian ruthlessness. Her father had been executed by Herod the Great and her husband had been named in one of Herod's earlier wills as his successor as King of Judea. No doubt the death-bed will was a severe blow to the ambitious Herodias. Notwithstanding the fate of her father and the misfortunes of her husband, Herodias did not appear to bear any ill will toward the house of Herod. Upon meeting Antipas, Herodias saw an opportunity to mitigate in some measure her disappointment over failing to become the Queen of Judea by becoming the wife of the Tetrarch of Galilee and Perea. As the wife of a tetrarch she might yet become a queen. Antipas was bewitched and an alliance was made.

Before any headway could be made Antipas had first to rid himself of the embarrassment of a wife of no mean heritage. She was the daughter of the King of Arabia. Notwithstanding his wife's high birthright, Antipas made secret plans to divorce her. Even in those days husbands could not keep secrets from their wives for long. Antipas' wife, learning of his plans, thoroughly outwitted him. Suggesting a holiday trip, she asked Antipas to permit her to go to Macherus (the castle where John the Baptist was later beheaded). To this Antipas readily agreed, no doubt grateful for the opportunity to have his wife out of the way while he completed his arrangements with Herodias. Macherus was near the border of Arabia and the so-called holiday became a flight to her father.[1]

It was at this time that the ministry of John the Baptist began. Josephus refers to John as a good man who

> commanded the Jews to exercise virtue, both as to right-eousness towards one another, and piety towards God, and so to come to baptism; for that the washing (with water) would be acceptable to him, if they made use of it, not in order to the putting away (or the remission) of some sins (only), but for the purification of the body; supposing still that the soul was thoroughly purified beforehand by righteousness. Now when (many) others came in crowds about him, for they were very greatly moved (or pleased) by hearing his words, Herod, who feared lest the great influence John had over the people might put it into his power and inclination to raise a rebellion, (for they seemed ready to do any thing he should advise,) thought it best, by putting him to death, to prevent any mischief he might cause, and not bring himself into difficulties, by sparing a man who might make him repent of it when it should be too late.[2]

Antipas' apprehensions over the possible political consequences of John's ministry were no doubt much aggravated by John's scathing attack on his marriage with Herodias. John denounced it as unlawful,[3] and unlawful it undoubtedly was.[4] The ultimate consequences of Herod's treatment of his wife and the execution of John almost led to disaster. Aretas, his father-in-law, declared war on him and utterly destroyed his armies.[5] The Jews attributed this destruction of the armies as a judgment of God on Herod for the execution of John.[6]

Throughout Jesus' lifetime blood continued to flow in Judea. Wars from without and rebellion and riots from within

63

never ceased. It is said that in the century during which Jesus lived 200,000 of the pick of the Jewish people perished either at the hands of their rulers or through internal strife.[7] Fear and intrigue reigned in the land. Spies were everywhere but courage was never dead. Through it all the Jews held fast to their religion. They looked to their God to deliver them. They believed that some day one of their race would arise to rule the whole world: a kingdom in which the truth of the Jewish religion would be declared and recognized. This produced two types of extremist: those who were prepared to compromise with evil, be it in their political or private lives, until the day of deliverance should arrive, just so long as the letter of the law was not breached; and those like the Zealots who were prepared to fight in the streets, in the hills and in the caves even against the greatest odds as long as any foreigner exercised authority over them. Never would they acknowledge the rule of Rome nor surrender to its legions. Nowhere were these gallant spirits more numerous than in the Tetrarchy of Herod Antipas, Galilee.

Herod had been annoyed by the restrictions imposed on him by Pilate, and when Pilate turned Jesus over to him for trial, his vanity was flattered by this mark of attention. Pilate had deferred to him in a jurisdictional matter and the opportunity to see and talk with the man of Galilee in some measure satisfied his curiosity. It was not the teaching of Jesus that provoked Herod's inquiring mind, but a desire to see him perform some miracle. So he questioned him at some length, but no answers were forthcoming. Jesus was exercising an elementary legal right when he remained silent. But his silence meant much more than that. If he had lifted his hand to gratify Herod's curiosity, he would have violated his whole divine mission on earth. If he had performed a miracle for Herod, he would have assumed the role of a magician.

64

Jesus well knew the character of the man before whom he was arraigned. Jesus had lived, worked and taught in Galilee. No man of his intellectual training could have helped knowing all about Herod. Had he not been threatened by the Pharisees: "Get away from here, for Herod wants to kill you"? To which he had replied with great aptness: "Go and tell that fox, 'Behold, I cast out demons and perform cures today and tomorrow, and the third day I finish my course.'" [8]

As the chief priests and scribes pursued their accusations with unabated venom, shrewd Herod saw an opportunity to gain favour with Pilate and at the same time ingratiate himself with the Jewish elders at Jerusalem. He was glad to evade consequences similar to those that flowed from the divorce of his wife. He continued to play his part in the drama by joining his bodyguards in abusing the prisoner. Bowing to Roman authority, he arrayed him "in gorgeous apparel," and "sent him back to Pilate." [9]

Pilate had paid his respects to Herod and Herod had paid his respects to Pilate. "And Herod and Pilate became friends with each other that very day, . . ." [10] The old sores that had been open since Pilate intermeddled with Herod's jurisdiction by mixing Galilean blood with their sacrifices[11] were healed.

X

THE SANHEDRISTS were not at the praetorium when the prisoner returned. "Pilate then called together the chief priests and the rulers and the people, . . ." [1] It is a fair inference that the rulers may have been detained in the temple to hear the confessions of Judas as he brought back the blood money. By now they were in no mood to hear any confessions that would tend to show the innocence of the prisoner on trial before Pilate. Judas said: "I have sinned in betraying innocent blood." [2] He probably knew the requirements of the Jewish law in capital cases that the court must hear any witness in favour of an acquittal even after judgment was rendered, as long as the sentence had not been carried out. If Judas did not know the law, the court most certainly did. Defying it they said: "What is that to us? See to it yourself." [3] With his legal right to be heard by the court denied, Judas threw down the tainted silver and went to his own destruction. The Sanhedrists were again seized with a fit of scrupulous scrupulosity. They would for their own ends disregard the law in a matter of life and death, but they were meticulous to observe it in a matter that was in comparison quite trivial. This money could not be taken into the treasury of the temple because it was the price of human blood. Since the money was obtained by unlawful means, it remained the money of Judas. [4] The thirty pieces of silver did not go into the temple treasury, but were used to buy an abandoned field where pottery had been made and to convert it into a burial ground for strangers. [5] Henceforth, this field was known as the Field of Blood. [6]

The Sanhedrists, having disposed of Judas, gathered again in Pilate's court where the case was reopened. Pilate addressed them: "You brought this man before me accusing him of treason. I have examined him in public before you. I find him not guilty of any of the charges against him. In that judgment I have been supported by Herod, who has sent him back to me." "Behold, nothing deserving death has been done by him; . . ." [7] For the second time the judgment delivered was clear and unequivocal. It was a finding that the prisoner was not guilty. The law demanded his release, and if Pilate had then released him, little could have been said or done. An acquittal by Pilate

66

would have been the final judicial word. But Pilate was a weak judge. As weak judges have done since the beginning of time, he equivocated—he temporized with justice and then compromised justice. Attempting to placate the emissaries of the Jews, he added a rider to his judgment: "I will therefore chastise him and release him." [8] Chastise him for what? Not for any offence that he had committed against the law but merely to satisfy a lust for vengeance.

The rider to the verdict was all that was needed. The Sanhedrists at once detected Pilate's vacillation as a concession. At this turn of the proceedings, which had rapidly lost all the character of a Roman trial, Claudia Procula, Pilate's wife, came on the stage to play her immortal part in the tragedy. Whether it be true or not that Claudia was a proselyte and as such may have known much more about Jesus and his teaching than appears in the record, she possessed a gentle-woman's sensitivity that stirs the soul to anguish in the face of injustice. To her husband she sent a message that was to give her a place in history for all time: "Have nothing to do with that righteous man, for I have suffered much over him today in a dream." [9] This message need not necessarily give rise to any speculation about mysticism. Dreams Claudia may have had. Much weight was put in the meaning of dreams in those days. Dreams were commonly considered a means of divine revelation and men endeavoured to induce prophetic dreams by sleeping potions. Such practices were followed by Mediterranean people and others, including Greeks and Romans.[10] No doubt Claudia well knew the course the events were taking and she knew as well that when passions enter the courtroom justice flies out. Not only passions but the mob spirit had entered the courtroom. The Sanhedrists excited the people to raise a chorus of death: "Away with this man, . . ."[11]

Once again shifting his ground, Pilate sought for a way

out. It was the custom that at every feast of the Passover the Roman governor should show a gesture of good will by releasing one prisoner condemned to death for a serious crime. There was in custody Barabbas, condemned for a murder committed in the course of an insurrection. Notwithstanding that Pilate had twice found Jesus not guilty, he now offered to release him, not as an innocent man, but as a convicted malefactor to whom an amnesty had been granted. Once again Pilate not only abrogated his judicial office but degraded the prerogative of mercy, a trust he held in the name of the emperor. The authority of Caesar was surrendered to the voice of the mob: "Which of the two do you want me to release ... ?" The mob replied: "Barabbas." [12] According to the law there was only one course open to Pilate to follow. Jesus had been found not guilty. He was entitled to be discharged and set free. For the second time Pilate surrendered his judicial functions to voices clamouring for violence. He appealed to the assembly: "Then what shall I do with the man whom you call the King of the Jews?" [13] Back from the mob came their answer: "Crucify him." [14] The judges of the Jewish court were now leading the rabble in shouting for a punishment unauthorized by Jewish law and of a such a nature as was forbidden expressly by Jewish law. Cruel as stoning, burning, beheading and strangling were, crucifixion was infinitely more cruel. Sometimes it took as much as three days for the victim to die. Pilate was still reluctant to give himself up to complete compliance with the spirit of the mob. He descended from the dais of judicial rectitude to argue with the disciples of violence: "Why, what evil has he done?" [15] The Sanhedrists were in no mood to argue. The only reply they made was: "Crucify him, crucify him." [16]

With Barabbas released, Pilate may have again seen a way of escape that would quench the thirst for the blood of the prisoner and at the same time save himself from any political repercussions. He delivered Jesus to the Roman soldiers to be scourged. It may be, however, that events were only taking their normal course following a sentence of death, as scourging was a Roman preliminary to crucifixion.[17] The soldiers, willing to make "a Roman holiday" for themselves, made a mockery of the whole proceedings. Arraying the prisoner in a purple robe and crowning him with a simulated crown woven from the twigs of thorn trees, they scourged him.[18]

The degradation of his office reached its culmination when Pilate entered into a sort of stage play. He went out again to the assembly of angry men and delivered another official judgment: "Behold, I am bringing him out to you, that you may know that I find no crime in him"—the third declaration of "not guilty." Each declaration was delivered with the authority, and in the name, of the emperor of all Rome by his procurator exercising his full legal power. To the verdict were added those words that were to be etched on the very souls of millions of human beings in centuries to come: "Behold the man!"[19] All this did nothing more than raise the chorus to a crescendo: "Crucify him, crucify him!"

Pilate beat his last evasive retreat: "Take him yourselves and crucify him, for I find no crime in him."[20] This declaration was the manifestation of either the traits of a fox or a villain, or both. It must have been known to Pilate that crucifixion was not a punishment permitted by Jewish law. Likewise, he must have known that capital punishment could not be inflicted unless the sentence was confirmed by him. One thing he made clear, he was not confirming the judgment of the Sanhedrin. For a fourth time Jesus had been acquitted of any crime worthy of death. If the Jews crucified Jesus on the basis on which Pilate was now disposing of the case, it would have been nothing less than murder. The Jews were not to be drawn into this trap. They at once brought Pilate back to the judicial function that they were insisting he perform. Having failed to secure a conviction for treason, the accusers fell back on a demand for confirmation of the death sentence passed by the Sanhedrin which was based on a conviction of blasphemy: ". . . he has made himself the Son of God." [21] Pilate was now in a new dilemma involving the religious affairs of the Jewish people which in the past had so often given rise to political turmoil. It may be he was remembering the injunction from Claudia when he again sought to question the prisoner privately:

Q. Where are you from?

No answer was forthcoming from the prisoner. All charges of treason having been disposed of, Jesus relied on his simple legal right to remain silent. A threatening question provoked an answer clothed with majesty:

Q. Do you not know that I have power to release you, and power to crucify you?
A. You would have no power over me unless it had been given you from above; therefore he who delivered me to you has the greater sin.[22]

This declaration is capable of a simple legal interpretation. Pilate exercised a delegated power conferred on him by Caesar. His only function was to confirm or refuse to confirm the judgment of the Jewish court. His power came from a higher authority—the emperor. The real sinners were those who falsely convicted Jesus in the courts of his own nation. Whatever the proper theological interpretation of the answer of Jesus may be, it is most likely that none other than the legal significance was apparent to Pilate. It brought him back to his responsibility as a judge in a Roman court. "Upon this Pilate sought to release him, . . ." [23] The ecclesiastical phalanx had not yet exhausted all their weapons. They still had a rapier well poisoned with Hebrew politics concealed in their robes. They knew their man and they knew his history. Again they remembered that Caesar had rebuked Pilate over the votive shields. Back they went to the charge of treason, not because there was any evidence to support it, but because the Sanhedrists knew how to strike Pilate in his weakest spot: "If you release this man, you are not Caesar's friend; every one who makes himself a king sets himself against Caesar."[24] Pilate's sensitivity to his record was well measured. He knew how hard it would be for him to answer to Tiberius on any charge that he had compromised with a Jew who was said to have asserted any temporal power in conflict with Roman authority. What had up to this time been a retreat on Pilate's part turned into absolute surrender. He brought Jesus out, stood him before the assembly and said: "Here is your King!" This raised the voice of the mob to its greatest pitch: "Away with him, away with him, crucify him!" With irony Pilate said: "Shall I crucify your King?" Back came a poisoned political arrow steeped in hypocrisy, but it was one that hit its mark: "We have no king but Caesar." Pilate no longer vacillated. He surrendered his judicial authority. Seeing a riot was beginning,[25] he handed the prisoner over to be crucified.[26] Violence had triumphed.

Probably out of contempt for the Jewish court, and, as some contend, to impress the Jewish people with the verdict of not guilty so repeatedly delivered but each time rejected by the Jewish authorities, Pilate adapted a Jewish rite to his own purposes. According to Jewish custom, where a murder was unsolved, the elders of the city nearest to the slain man took a young heifer into a rough, uncultivated valley and cut off its head: "And all the elders of that city nearest to the slain man shall wash their hands over the heifer whose neck was broken in the valley; and they shall testify, 'Our hands did not shed this blood, neither did our eyes see it shed.' " [27] And so, Pilate "took water and washed his hands before the crowd, saying, 'I am innocent of this man's blood; see to it yourselves.' And all the people answered, 'His blood be on us and on our children!' " [28]

The whole catalogue of illegality was complete; Jesus Christ, the prisoner, had been betrayed to his enemies for thirty pieces of silver; beaten and tortured by his custodians; illegally tried in the highest court of his nation; illegally convicted of blasphemy against the God of his people—a conviction never confirmed in the Roman court. Confirmation failing, the prisoner was charged with treason against the Roman emperor and found not guilty; nevertheless he was "handed over to be crucified." In all the annals of legal history, it would be difficult to find another case in which a prisoner who had been declared not guilty by a court of competent jurisdiction was delivered to the executioner by the judge who had acquitted him.

A whole battalion of soldiers was called together to carry out the execution. Mark puts the scourging at this stage of the proceedings. This may be correct or Jesus may have been scourged twice.

> And they clothed him in a purple cloak, and plaiting a crown of thorns they put it on him. And they began to salute him, 'Hail, King of the Jew!' And they struck his head with a reed, and spat upon him, and they knelt down in homage to him. And when they had mocked him, they stripped him of the purple cloak, and put his own clothes on him. And they led him out to crucify him.[29]

As a deterrent to others it was the custom to affix to the

cross a board on which was inscribed the offence for which the condemned man had been convicted. This board was carried before the prisoner as he was taken to the place of execution. In this case Pilate himself prepared the inscription. It was written in Latin, Greek and Aramaic. It read: "The King of the Jews." [30] The chief priests soon learned of what Pilate had written and they sought him out and protested. There is real legal significance in this manœuvre and it is quite clear what it is. The chief priests asked Pilate to change the inscription to read: "This man said, 'I am King of the Jews.' " [31] If Pilate had stated the offence for which Jesus was crucified as the chief priests asked, it would have meant that Jesus had been found guilty of treason. This was a judgment Pilate had persistently refused to pass. He had simply handed Jesus over to be crucified. Pilate rejected the demands of the Sanhedrists and closed the case with a simple statement: "What I have written I have written."

XI

IT WAS a very different procession that made its way from the Antonia to the "place of a skull" outside the walls than that which had wended its way from Bethpage down over the slopes of the Mount of Olives through the Garden of Gethsemane to the temple gate just five days before. All who had strewn palm leaves in the path of Jesus, except a few "acquaintances and the women who had followed him from Galilee," [1] had forsaken him and fled.

The right under Jewish law to be executed without any

form of torture was denied the prisoner until the last. Notwithstanding that he had been beaten and scourged, he was now required to carry his cross to the place of execution, but the burden was too great. He stumbled and fell. A casual visitor to the feast of the Passover was pressed into service, one Simon from the Jewish settlement of Cyrene in North Africa.[2] Little did that casual visitor know that his impressment was to give immortality to his name.

Certain women in the melancholy entourage defied the Jewish law that there should be no lamentation for one sentenced to death.[3] These women followed the condemned man, weeping. To them Jesus said: "Daughters of Jerusalem, do not weep for me, but weep for yourselves and for your children." [4] Then he repeated a prophecy made a few days before at the temple,[5] and quoted from the words of Hosea.[6] For the Jews this prophecy was to come true all too soon, even during the lives of those then living, and in this atomic age it may yet come true for all mankind:

> For behold, the days are coming when they will say, "Blessed are the barren, and the wombs that never bore, and the breasts that never gave suck!" Then they will begin to say to the mountains, "Fall on us"; and to the hills, "Cover us." For if they do this when the wood is green, what will happen when it is dry? [7]

Arriving at the place of execution the Roman soldiers addressed themselves to their gruesome task. Just where the exact spot of execution was is a matter of dispute among scholars and archeologists. The Church of the Holy Sepulchre is said to mark the place; others contend that the lovely little garden known as "Gordon's Calvary" is the place, but does it matter? That it would be a place outside the walls is certain,

74

as by Jewish law executions were not permitted within the walls, but where the walls were at that time is not yet settled.

Crucifixion was the most horrible of all punishments. It is Oriental in origin and said to have been borrowed by the Romans from the Carthaginians. It was reserved for slaves and subjects of occupied territories. A Roman citizen was not subject to crucifixion. So painful was the torture that it gave birth to a word to express the extremity of anguish—*cruciatus,* whence comes the English word "excruciating." [8] The victim's hands and feet were made fast to the cross, usually by nails, sometimes by thongs. He might hang two or three days or more before life was extinguished.

There was a humane custom among the Jews to give one sentenced to death a sedative potion to dull the pain. "Give strong drink to him who is perishing, and wine to those in bitter distress; . . ." [9] It is said that there was a society of charitable ladies in Jerusalem who prepared this merciful potion.[10] Doubtless this was the wine "mingled with gall" that was offered to Jesus and which he tasted and refused.[11]

So Jesus was crucified and with him two robbers, one on the right and one on the left.[12] But the chief priests, scribes and elders were not through with him yet. It was not enough that they should destroy his life; they were also determined to destroy any legacy that he might leave to mankind. They came to the scene and ". . . mocked him, saying, 'He saved others; he cannot save himself. He is the King of Israel; let him come down now from the cross, and we will believe in him. He trusts in God; let God deliver him now, if he desires him; for he said, "I am the Son of God." ' "[13] Mockery failed utterly in its purpose. The mockers and the mockery have all been swallowed up in the oblivion of centuries, but Jesus' answer to those who mocked him and those who crucified him lives timelessly in the hearts of devoted men and women every-where in the world. Times without number his answer has been on the prayerful lips of dying martyrs: "Father, forgive them; for they know not what they do." [14]

At the ninth hour Jesus was dead. The sun had not yet gone down. The Sabbath and the feast of the Passover had not yet commenced. All was accomplished. In lesser matters the letter of the law had been observed. It remained for the commander of the Roman guard to give the final verdict on the day's miscarriage of justice:

Certainly this man was innocent![15]

EPILOGUE

THE PRINCIPAL characters—Caiaphas, Annas, Herod Antipas and Pontius Pilate—all played their parts and left the stage, each to the misery of his own destiny.

Caiaphas disappeared from the scene, condemned by his own people. When Vitellius became Legate to Syria, he ordered the vestments of the high priests, which had been kept in the custody of the captain of the Roman guard at the Antonia, to be transferred to the Jews "as an act of kindness, to oblige the nation to him. Besides which, he also deprived Joseph, who was called Caiaphas, of the high priesthood, . . ."[1]

Old Annas lived to see the oppression of the Romans outmatched by the cruelty of the Jewish people to one another. All semblance of internal order broke down. Revolt and rebellion developed into a bloody civil war. ". . . those people that were the dearest to one another broke through all restraints with regard to each other, and every one associated with those of his own opinion, and began already to stand in opposition one to another; . . ."[2] Robber bands developed into veritable robber armies. The barbarity that the Jewish people suffered at the hands of their own was worse than that suffered at the hands of the Romans. ". . . it seemed to be a much lighter thing to be ruined by the Romans than by themselves."[3]

77

The leading citizens were seized and slaughtered in prison,[4] and Jerusalem became a city without a governor where murder and rapine were rife and famine reared its ugly head. The robber army of Zealots seized the temple with all its sacred treasures and converted it into a fortress. The high priest was deposed and the office disposed of by lot to ignoble ruffians.[5]

Annas put himself at the head of a band of citizens who engaged the Zealots in a bitter struggle. The Zealots called to their assistance an Idumean army that was, if anything, more reckless in bloodshed than the Zealots had been. The resisting Jews "were driven one upon another in heaps, so were they slain. . . . And now the outer temple was all of it overflowed with blood; . . ."[6] Annas was slain and an Idumean soldier stood on his dead body and upbraided him "with his kindness to the people, . . ."[7] Notwithstanding the Machiavellian part Annas had played to dispose of Jesus, no one can deny that when his time came he met death with great courage.

Herod Antipas suffered the curse of being married to ambitious Herodias, and it was that unlawful alliance that proved to be his destruction. When Caius succeeded Tiberius as Emperor of Rome, he raised Herodias' brother Agrippa, a friend of his youth, to the rank of King of the Tetrarchy of Philip. He also "changed his iron chain for a golden one of equal weight," and "put a diadem upon his head."[8] Not only had Agrippa been a mere private citizen, but he had been held prisoner by Tiberius because he had been overheard expressing a wish that Tiberius would soon pass off the stage and leave the government to his friend Caius, saying he was in every respect more worthy of it.[9]

Agrippa's sudden good fortune was more than Herodias' envious disposition could endure. Was it not true that her brother had fled to Rome to escape his creditors? Now he returned to his native land, a king, while her husband was still a mere tetrarch. Josephus describes in picturesque language Herodias' domestic grievances which were to end in utter misfortune for both herself and Herod:

> She was therefore grieved and much displeased at so great a mutation of his [Agrippa's] affairs; and chiefly when she saw him marching among the multitude with the usual ensigns of royal authority, she was not able to conceal how miserable she was, by reason of the envy she had towards him; but she excited her husband and desired him that he would sail to Rome, to court honours equal to his; for she said that she could not bear to live any longer, while Agrippa, the son of that Aristobulus who was condemned to die by his father, one that came to her husband in such extreme poverty, that the necessaries of life were forced to be entirely supplied him day by day; and when he fled away from his creditors by sea, he now returned a king; . . .[10]

Antipas set off for Rome counselled by his wife: ". . . let us spare no pains nor expenses, either of silver or gold, since they cannot be kept for any better use than for obtaining a kingdom."[11] Agrippa did not take kindly to his sister's ambitions. Learning of the expedition to Rome and its purpose, he dispatched a confidential messenger to Caius "to carry presents" and letters accusing Herod of being a party to a treasonable conspiracy against the government of Caius in Judea. Caius believed the accusation and deprived Herod of his tetrarchy which he added to Agrippa's kingdom. The property of both Herod and Herodias was forfeited and given to Agrippa, and Herod was banished for life to Lyons "a city of Gaul."[12]

No matter how evil a person may be it is rare that there is not some element of good in him, and Herodias was no exception. When Caius learned that Herodias was Agrippa's sister, he remitted his order that her money be forfeited and told her that it was her brother who had saved her from the same fate as her husband. To this she replied: "Thou, indeed, O emperor! actest after a magnificent manner, and as becomes thyself, in what thou offerest me; but the kindness which I have for my husband hinders me from partaking of the favour of thy gift; for it is not just that I, who have been made a partner in his prosperity, should forsake him in his misfortunes." With a courage and devotion that one would not have expected of her, Herodias elected to be condemned to banishment with her husband.

Josephus concludes his account of the evil career of Herod Antipas and his equally evil wife: "And thus did God punish Herodias for her envy at her brother, and Herod also for giving ear to the vain discourses of a woman." [13] So ended the man who mocked Jesus and sent him back to Pilate.

Pilate passed into oblivion. The last account that authentic history records of him is his recall to Rome just at the time Tiberius died. The events leading to his recall were as follows. The Samaritans believed that the sacred utensils of the temple had remained buried on the mountain of Gerizim since Moses' time. When an imposter assembled a large gathering to ascend the mountain to be shown the treasures, Pilate sent an army which killed a great many of them, arrested others and condemned their leaders to death. As many of those assembled were armed, it would not be unreasonable to assume that they were bent on insurrection. The whole occurrence was not an unusual one, but upon hearing of it, Vitellius, the Legate of

Syria, to whom Pilate was responsible, ordered him to return to Rome and turn over the administration of Judea to Marcellus.[14]

The record of the subsequent fortunes of Pilate is obscure. The Christian writers Eusebius and Orosius attribute his death to suicide either in Rome or Vienna to which he was said to have been banished.[15]

Where justice is destroyed by injustice, or truth by falsehood, while the judges look on, there they shall also be destroyed.

LAWS OF MANU

NOTES

I

[1] Flavius Josephus, *Antiquities of the Jews*, trans. William Whiston (Philadelphia: John C. Winston Co., 1957) Book XVIII, Chapter 2: paragraph 2.

II

[1] Flavius Josephus, *Antiquities of the Jews*, trans. William Whiston (Philadelphia: John C. Winston Co., 1957) Book XIV.

[2] Flavius Josephus, *Wars of the Jews*, trans. William Whiston (Philadelphia: John C. Winston Co., 1957) Book I, Chapter 7: paragraph 5.

[3] Josephus, *Antiquities*, XIV, 9: 2.

[4] Alfred Edersheim, *The Life and Times of Jesus the Messiah* (New York: E. R. Herrick & Company, 1886) I, p. 217.

[5] Josephus, *Antiquities*, XVII, 6: 2 ff.

[6] Josephus, *Wars*, I, 23: 7.

[7] Josephus, *Antiquities*, XVII, 8: 2.

[8] *Ibid.*, 9: 3.

[9] Josephus, *Wars*, II, 1: 3.

[10] Josephus, *Antiquities*, XVII, 9: 5.

[11] *Ibid.*, 1-7.

[12] *Ibid.*, 7.

[13] Edersheim, *op. cit.*, I, pp. 11 and 220; Josephus, *Wars*, II, 5: 1-7.

[14] Josephus, *Antiquities*, XVII, 8: 1.

[15] Stewart Perowne, *The Later Herods* (London: Hodder and Stoughton Limited, 1958) p. 16.

[16] Josephus, *Antiquities*, XVII, 10: 2.

[17] *Ibid.*, 8.
[18] *Ibid.*, 10.
[19] *Ibid.*, 13: 2.
[20] *Ibid.*, XVIII, 6: 5.

III

[1] Matt. 5: 20, Revised Standard Version (New York: Thomas Nelson & Sons, 1952).

[2] Luke 5: 17 (R.S.V.).

[3] Alfred Edersheim, *The Life and Times of Jesus the Messiah* (New York: E. R. Herrick & Company, 1886) I, p. 93.

[4] *Ibid.*, p. 94.

[5] Joseph Klausner, *Jesus of Nazareth: His Life, Times and Teaching*, trans. Herbert Danby (New York: The Macmillan Company, 1957) p. 201.

[6] Flavius Josephus, *Antiquities of the Jews*, trans. William Whiston (Philadelphia: John C. Winston Co., 1957) Book XVII, Chapter 2: paragraph 4.

[7] *Ibid.*, XIII, 16: 2.

[8] *Ibid.*, XVIII, 1: 3.

[9] Emil Schürer, *A History of the Jewish People in the Time of Jesus Christ* (Edinburgh: T. & T. Clark, 1890) II: 2, pp. 24 and 25.

[10] Josephus, *Antiquities*, XIII, 10: 6.

[11] *Ibid.*, 10: 5; XVII, 2: 4.

[12] Edersheim, *op. cit.*, I, p. 312.

[13] Josephus, *Antiquities*, XVII, 2: 4.

[14] *Ibid.*, XVIII, 1: 3.

[15] Acts 5: 17 (R.S.V.).

[16] Josephus, *Antiquities*, XX, 9: 1.

[17] Edersheim, *op. cit.*, I, p. 322.

[18] *Ibid.*, p. 314.

[19] Josephus, *Antiquities*, XVIII, 1: 4; Schürer, *op. cit.*, II: 2, p. 38.

[20] Schürer, *op. cit.*, II: 2, p. 34.

[21] *Ibid.*, II: 2, p. 42; Josephus, *Antiquities*, XVIII, 1: 4.

[22] For a discussion of these differences see Edersheim, *op. cit.*, I, p. 319.

[1] Sanhedrin, Chapter 7: paragraph 8, *The Mishnah*, trans. Herbert Danby (London: Oxford University Press, 1954).

[2] Num. 15: 32-36, Revised Standard Version (New York: Thomas Nelson & Sons, 1952).

[3] Matt. 12: 2; Mark 2: 23 (R.S.V.).

[4] I Sam. 21: 1-6 (R.S.V.).

[5] Num. 28: 9-10 (R.S.V.).

[6] Joseph Klausner, *Jesus of Nazareth: His Life, Times and Teaching*, trans. Herbert Danby (New York: The Macmillan Company, 1957) p. 278.

[7] Mark 3: 6 (R.S.V.).

[8] Alfred Edersheim, *The Life and Times of Jesus the Messiah* (New York: E. R. Herrick & Company, 1886) I, pp. 237-40 and II, p. 284; Klausner, *op. cit.*, p. 279.

[9] Matt. 13: 54 (R.S.V.).

[10] *Ibid.*, 14: 1.

[11] *Ibid.*, 15: 2.

[12] *Ibid.*, 7-9.

[13] *Ibid.*, 10.

[14] *Ibid.*, 12.

[15] *Ibid.*, 13 and 14.

[16] *Ibid.*, 17, 18, 19 and 20.

[17] *Ibid.*, 16: 1.

[18] Ex. 22: 18; Deut. 18: 20 (R.S.V.).

[19] Sanhedrin, 7: 4.

[20] *Ibid.*, 11: 5.

[21] Matt. 16: 3-4 (R.S.V.).

[22] *Ibid.*, 21.

[23] Luke 18: 31 (R.S.V.).

[24] Matt. 19: 3 (R.S.V.).

[25] *Ibid.*, 4-6. See also Gen. 1: 27 and 28, and 2: 24 (R.S.V.).

[26] Deut. 24: 1 (R.S.V.).

[27] Flavius Josephus, *Wars of the Jews*, trans. William Whiston (Philadelphia: John C. Winston Co., 1957) Book IV, Chapter 8: paragraph 3; Edersheim, *op. cit.*, 11, p. 350.

[28] Luke 19: 7 (R.S.V.).

29 *Ibid.*, 8.
30 Lev. 6: 1-5; Num. 5: 6-7 (R.S.V.).
31 David Smith, *The Days of His Flesh* (New York: George H. Doran Company, n.d.) p. 386 and footnote.
32 I Kings 17: 3 (R.S.V.).
33 John 11: 47 and 48 (R.S.V.).
34 *Ibid.*, 50.
35 *Ibid.*, 53.
36 Smith, *op. cit.*, p. 387.
37 Luke 7: 36 (R.S.V.).
38 See Smith, *op. cit.*, p. 204.
39 Mark 14: 3 (R.S.V.).
40 John 12: 6 (R.S.V.).
41 Mark 14: 9 (R.S.V.).
42 Smith, *op. cit.*, p. 389.

V

1 Zech. 9: 9, Revised Standard Version (New York: Thomas Nelson & Sons, 1952).
2 Jer. 7: 11 (R.S.V.).
3 Matt. 21: 23 (R.S.V.).
4 *Ibid.*, 23-27; Mark 11: 27-33 (R.S.V.).
5 Matt. 21: 31-32 and 43 (R.S.V.).
6 *Ibid.*, 45.
7 *Ibid.*, 22: 15 and 16.
8 *Ibid.*, 17.
9 *Ibid.*, 21.
10 Deut. 25: 5 and 6 (R.S.V.). See also Yebamoth, Chapter 2: paragraph 2, *The Mishnah*, trans. Herbert Danby (London: Oxford University Press, 1954).
11 Matt. 22: 24-28 (R.S.V.).
12 *Ibid.*, 30.
13 *Ibid.*, 36.
14 *Ibid.*, 37. See also Deut. 6: 5 (R.S.V.).
15 Matt. 22: 39 (R.S.V.). See also Lev. 19: 18 (R.S.V.).
16 Matt. 22: 46 (R.S.V.).
17 *Ibid.*, 23: 1-5. See also Deut. 11: 18; 6: 4-9; 11: 13-21 (R.S.V.).

18 Matt. 23: 6-7 (R.S.V.).

19 *Ibid.*, 15-19.

20 *Ibid.*, 23-33.

21 *Ibid.*, 26: 4.

22 *Ibid.*, 3-5.

23 He was a Judean. Alfred Edersheim, *The Life and Times of Jesus the Messiah* (New York: E. R. Herrick & Company, 1886) I, p. 522.

24 Luke 22: 6 (R.S.V.).

25 Matt. 26: 48 (R.S.V.).

26 *Ibid.*, 49-50.

27 *Ibid.*, 55.

VI

1 David Smith, *The Days of His Flesh* (New York: George H. Doran Company, n.d.) p. 463, quoting from Lightfoot on John 18: 13.

2 *The Life of Flavius Josephus*, trans. William Whiston (Philadelphia: John C. Winston Co., 1957) paragraph 12.

3 Flavius Josephus, *Antiquities of the Jews*, trans. William Whiston (Philadelphia: John C. Winston Co., 1957) Book XVIII, Chapter 2: paragraph 2.

4 It was Annas the younger who presided over the judicial murder of James, the brother of Jesus. This Annas was a Sadducee. He was "very rigid in judging offenders, above all the rest of the Jews, . . ." (Josephus, *Antiquities*, XX, 9: 1.) In the absence of Albinus, the Roman governor, Annas the younger summoned James and some others before the Sanhedrin to stand their trial as "breakers of the law." In due course they were sentenced to be stoned. This was quite illegal. It cost Annas his office. Right-minded citizens not only protested to King Agrippa but went all the way to Alexandria to lodge their complaint personally with Albinus who was vacationing there. Albinus "wrote in anger to Ananus," and threatened him with punishment for what he had done. He was thereupon released from the office he had held for only three months. (Josephus, *Antiquities*, XX, 9: 1.) In due course he himself was to suffer death at the hands of the people. (Emil Schürer, *A History of the Jewish People in the Time of Jesus Christ*, II: 1, p. 201.)

86

[5] Josephus, *Antiquities*, p. 599 footnote.

[6] *Ibid.*, XX, 9: 2.

[7] Werner Keller, *The Bible as History* (New York: W. W. Morrow, 1957) p. 372.

[8] Emil Schürer, *A History of the Jewish People in the Time of Jesus Christ* (Edinburgh: T. & T. Clark, 1890) II: 1, pp. 230 ff.

[9] A. Taylor Innes, *The Trial of Jesus Christ* (Edinburgh: T. & T. Clark, 1899) p. 25, quoting Salvador's *Institutes*, p. 366.

[10] John 18: 19-24, Revised Standard Version (New York: Thomas Nelson & Sons, 1952).

VII

[1] Num. 11: 16, Revised Standard Version (New York: Thomas Nelson & Sons, 1952).

[2] Emil Schürer, *A History of the Jewish People in the Time of Jesus Christ* (Edinburgh: T. & T. Clark, 1890) II: 1, p. 166.

[3] John Henry Wigmore, *Panorama of World Legal Systems* (St. Paul: West Publishing Company, 1928) I, p. 112.

[4] *Ibid.*, p. 113.

[5] *Ibid.*

[6] Schürer, *op. cit.*, II: 1, p. 168.

[7] Flavius Josephus, *Antiquities of the Jews*, trans. William Whiston (Philadelphia: John C. Winston Co., 1957) Book XIV, Chapter 9: paragraph 4.

[8] Schürer, *op. cit.*, II: 1, p. 187.

[9] Sanhedrin, Chapter 4: paragraph 4, *The Mishnah*, trans. Herbert Danby (London: Oxford University Press, 1954).

[10] Lev. 24: 16 (R.S.V.).

[11] Num. 15: 32-36 (R.S.V.); Sanhedrin, 7: 8.

[12] Deut. 18: 10 (R.S.V.).

[13] *Ibid.*, 13: 6-11; Sanhedrin, 7: 10.

[14] *Ibid.*, 18: 20; Sanhedrin, 7: 7.

[15] Sanhedrin, 7: 1.

[16] *Ibid.*, 9: 4.

[17] *Ibid.*, 5: 2.

[18] *Ibid.*, 4: 5.

[19] Deut. 17: 6 (R.S.V.); Makkoth, Chapter 1: paragraph 7,

The Mishnah, trans. Herbert Danby (London: Oxford University Press, 1954).

[20] Deut. 19: 19 (R.S.V.) ; Makkoth, 14: 5.

[21] Sanhedrin, 5: 2.

[22] *Ibid.,* 4.

[23] *Ibid.,* 4 ff.

[24] Makkoth, 1: 10.

[25] Lev. 24: 14 (R.S.V.).

[26] Sanhedrin, 6: 1.

[27] *Ibid.*

[28] Deut. 17: 7 (R.S.V.) ; Sanhedrin, 6: 4.

[29] Matt. 26: 59 (R.S.V.).

[30] Mark 14: 57-58 (R.S.V.).

[31] *Ibid.,* 56-59.

[32] A. Taylor Innes, *The Trial of Jesus Christ* (Edinburgh: T. & T. Clark, 1899) p. 42.

[33] *Ibid.,* pp. 45 ff.

[34] *Ibid.,* p. 25.

[35] *Ibid.,* p. 41.

[36] Matt. 26: 63-64 (R.S.V.).

[37] Mark 14: 62 (R.S.V.).

[38] Luke 22: 67-70 (R.S.V.).

[39] Sanhedrin, 7: 5.

[40] Matt. 26: 65-66 (R.S.V.).

[41] *Ibid.,* 66.

[42] Alfred Edersheim, *The Life and Times of Jesus the Messiah* (New York: E. R. Herrick & Company, 1886) II, p. 563.

[43] Matt. 27: 1; Mark 15: 1; Luke 23: 1; John 18: 28 (R.S.V.).

[44] Taylor Innes, *op. cit.,* p. 56.

[45] Amos 5: 24 (R.S.V.).

[46] Micah 6: 8, Authorized King James Version (New York: Oxford University Press, n.d.).

VIII

[1] Emil Schürer, *A History of the Jewish People in the Time of Jesus Christ* (Edinburgh: T. & T. Clark, 1890) I: 2, pp. 82-83, quoting from Philo, *De Legatione ad Cajum,* sec. 38.

² Abodah Zarah, Chapter 3: paragraph 1, *The Mishnah*, trans. Herbert Danby (London: Oxford University Press, 1954).

³ Flavius Josephus, *Antiquities of the Jews*, trans. William Whiston (Philadelphia: John C. Winston Co., 1957) Book XVIII, Chapter 3: paragraph 1; Josephus, *Wars of the Jews*, trans. William Whiston (Philadelphia: John C. Winston Co., 1957) Book II, Chapter 9: paragraphs 1 ff. See also Schürer, *op. cit.*, I: 2, p. 83.

⁴ Josephus, *Antiquities*, XVIII, 3: 2; *Wars*, II, 9: 4.

⁵ Luke 13: 1, Revised Standard Version (New York: Thomas Nelson & Sons, 1952).

⁶ David Smith, *The Days of His Flesh* (New York: George H. Doran Company, n.d.) p. 479.

⁷ John 18: 28 (R.S.V.).

⁸ *Ibid.*, 29.

⁹ *Ibid.*, 30.

¹⁰ *Ibid.*, 31. When Paul was brought before Gallio to stand trial on a charge that he was "persuading men to worship God contrary to the law," Gallio said, "If it were a matter of wrongdoing or vicious crime, I should have reason to bear with you, O Jews; but since it is a matter of questions about words and names and your own law, see to it yourselves; I refuse to be a judge of these things." (Acts 18: 13-17, R.S.V.).

¹¹ Luke 23: 2 (R.S.V.).

¹² A. Taylor Innes, *The Trial of Jesus Christ* (Edinburgh: T. & T. Clark, 1899) p. 85.

¹³ Smith, *op. cit.*, p. 485.

¹⁴ John 18: 33-34 (R.S.V.).

¹⁵ *Ibid.*, 35.

¹⁶ *Ibid.*, 36 ff.

¹⁷ *Ibid.*, 37.

¹⁸ *Ibid.*

¹⁹ *Ibid.*, 38.

²⁰ Luke 23: 4 (R.S.V.).

²¹ Josephus, *Antiquities*, XVIII, 3: 2.

²² Luke 23: 5 (R.S.V.).

²³ *Ibid.*, 6 and 7.

IX

[1] Flavius Josephus, *Antiquities of the Jews*, trans. William Whiston (Philadelphia: John C. Winston Co., 1957) Book XVIII, Chapter 5: paragraph 1.

[2] *Ibid.*, 2.

[3] Matt. 14: 3 and 4; Mark 6: 17 and 18, Revised Standard Version (New York: Thomas Nelson & Sons, 1952).

[4] Lev. 18: 16 (R.S.V.).

[5] Josephus, *Antiquities*, XVIII, 5: 1; Emil Schürer, *A History of the Jewish People in the Time of Jesus Christ* (Edinburgh: T. & T. Clark, 1890) I: 2, pp. 20 ff.

[6] Josephus, *Antiquities*, XVIII, 5: 2.

[7] Joseph Klausner, *Jesus of Nazareth: His Life, Times and Teaching*, trans. Herbert Danby (New York: The Macmillan Company, 1957) p. 167.

[8] Luke 13: 31 and 32 (R.S.V.).

[9] *Ibid.*, 23: 11.

[10] *Ibid.*, 12.

[11] *Ibid.*, 13: 1.

X

[1] Luke 23: 13, Revised Standard Version (New York: Thomas Nelson & Sons, 1952).

[2] Matt. 27: 4 (R.S.V.).

[3] *Ibid.*

[4] Alfred Edersheim, *The Life and Times of Jesus the Messiah* (New York: E. R. Herrick & Company, 1886) II, p. 575.

[5] Matt. 26: 6 and 7 (R.S.V.).

[6] Acts 1: 16-19 (R.S.V.).

[7] Luke 23: 14 and 15 (R.S.V.).

[8] *Ibid.*, 16.

[9] Matt. 27: 19 (R.S.V.).

[10] *The New Schaff-Herzog Encyclopaedia of Religious Knowledge* (Grand Rapids: Baker Book House, 1949-50) IV, 2. See also Num. 12: 6; Deut. 13: 1-5; I Sam. 28: 6-15 (R.S.V.).

[11] Luke 23: 18 (R.S.V.).

[12] Matt. 27: 21 (R.S.V.).

[13] Mark 15: 12 (R.S.V.).

[14] *Ibid.*, 13.

[15] *Ibid.*, 14.

[16] *Ibid.*, 13.

[17] Flavius Josephus, *Wars of the Jews*, trans. William Whiston (Philadelphia: John C. Winston Co., 1957) Book II, Chapter 14: paragraph 9; Book V, Chapter 11: paragraph 1.

[18] The convent of the Sisters of Notre-Dame de Sion rests today on the site of the Antonia. There one may see in the crypt the paving stones on which Jesus stood as he was scourged and mocked. Detail of diagrams for games played by Roman soldiers with dice can be seen etched in the flagstones. One of these games was "the game of King." A burlesque king was chosen and loaded with spurious honours, only to be put to death at the end of the farce. The luck of the game determined the unfortunate one who was to be king.

[19] John 19: 5, Authorized King James Version (New York: Oxford University Press, n.d.).

[20] John 19: 6 (R.S.V.).

[21] *Ibid.*, 7.

[22] *Ibid.*, 10 and 11.

[23] *Ibid.*, 12.

[24] *Ibid.*

[25] Matt. 27: 27 (R.S.V.).

[26] John 19: 16 (R.S.V.).

[27] Deut. 21: 1-7 (R.S.V.). See also Psalms 26: 6 and 73: 13 (R.S.V.).

[28] Matt. 27: 24 and 25 (R.S.V.).

[29] Mark 15: 16-20 (R.S.V.).

[30] *Ibid.*, 26.

[31] John 19: 21 (R.S.V.).

XI

[1] Luke 23: 49, Revised Standard Version (New York: Thomas Nelson & Sons, 1952).

[2] Mark 15: 21 (R.S.V.).

[3] David Smith, *The Days of His Flesh* (New York: George H. Doran Company, n.d.) p. 493, referring to Lightfoot on Matthew.

[4] Luke 23: 28 (R.S.V.).

[5] *Ibid.*, 21: 23.

[6] Hosea 10: 8 (R.S.V.).
[7] Luke 23: 29-31 (R.S.V.).
[8] Smith, *op. cit.*, p. 494.
[9] Prov. 31: 6 (R.S.V.).
[10] Smith, *op. cit.*, p. 495.
[11] Matt. 27: 34 (R.S.V.).
[12] *Ibid.*, 38.
[13] *Ibid.*, 41-43.
[14] Luke 23: 34 (R.S.V.).
[15] *Ibid.*, 47.

Epilogue

[1] Flavius Josephus, *Antiquities of the Jews*, trans. William Whiston (Philadelphia: John C. Winston Co., 1957) Book XVIII, Chapter 4: paragraph 3.

[2] Flavius Josephus, *Wars of the Jews*, trans. William Whiston (Philadelphia: John C. Winston Co., 1957) Book IV, Chapter 3: paragraph 2.

[3] *Ibid.*

[4] *Ibid.*, 5.

[5] *Ibid.*, 7.

[6] *Ibid.*, 5: 1.

[7] *Ibid.*, 2.

[8] Josephus, *Antiquities*, XVIII, 6: 10.

[9] *Ibid.*, 5.

[10] *Ibid.*, 7: 1.

[11] *Ibid.*

[12] *Ibid.*, 2.

[13] *Ibid.*

[14] *Ibid.*, 4: 2.

[15] Emil Schürer, *A History of the Jewish People in the Time of Jesus Christ* (Edinburgh: T. & T. Clark, 1890) I: 2, p. 87; Stewart Perowne, *The Later Herods* (London: Hodder and Stoughton Limited, 1958) p. 54.

INDEX

93

John, 52
John the Baptist, 20, 31, 58, 62, **63**
Josephus: quoted, 12, 16, 17, 40, 63, 79, 80
Joshua, 23, 24
Judas (Rabbi), 7-8, 9
Judas Iscariot, 27, 37, 38, 65-6
Julia, 11

levirate marriage, 33-4
Luke, 50, 55

Maccabean Wars, 4
Maccabees, 4, 16
Macherus, 62
Malchus, 3, 38
Malthake, 8
Marcellus, 81
Mariamne, 8
Mark, 50, 72
Mark Antony, 6, 24
Mary (harlot), 27
Matthias, 7-8, 9
Moses, 17, 19, 23, 24, 34, 43, 48, 80

Nicolaus, 10

parables: good Samaritan, 26; two sons in vineyard, 31; wicked husbandmen, 32
Passover, 3, 9, 10, 24, 28, 36, 37, 39, 55, 62, 68, 74, 76
Peter, 21, 25, 38, 41, 52, 59
Pharisees, 14, 15-16, 16-17, 18, 19, 20, 21, 23, 26, 32, 33, 34, 35, 65

Philip, 8, 11, 62, 78
Pompey, 5
Pontius Pilate, 22, 39, 40, 52, 53-6, 57, 58, 59, 60, 61, 64, 65, 66, 67, 68, 69, 70, 71, 72, 73, 77, 80-1

Roman law, 56, 60; offences, 57; procedure, 56, 57, 58; punishment, 56, 69, 75

Sabinius, 12
Sadducees, 14, 15, 16, 17, 18, 19, 21, 33, 34
St. Chrysostom, 27-8
Salome, 8
Sanhedrin, 5, 15, 26, 28, 42, 43-4, 47, 49, 50, 51, 52, 55, 56, 57, 59, 69, 70
Sanhedrists, 58, 60, 61, 65, 66, 67, 68, 71, 73
scribes, 14, 15, 17, 20, 22, 34, 35
Simon (healed leper), 27, 28
Simon (Pharisee), 27
Simon of Cyrene, 74
Solomon, 4, 7

Talmud, 41
Tiberius, 13, 53, 54, 55, 57, 58, 60, 68, 70, 71, 78, 80
Torah, 18

Varus, 12, 13
Vitellius, 40, 77, 80-1

Zacchaeus, 24-5, 26, 27, 58
Zealots, 7, 15, 16, 64, 78